Tim
Rodda

2 95

PGG

THANK GOD, I'M OK

D1211399

THANK GOD I'M OK

the gospel according to t.a.

Richard A. Batey

Abingdon   Nashville

THANK GOD, I'M OK:

The Gospel According to T.A.

Copyright © 1976 by Abingdon

All rights reserved
No part of this book may be reproduced in any manner whatsoever without written permission of the
publisher except brief quotations embodied in critical
articles or reviews. For information address Abingdon,
Nashville, Tennessee.

Library of Congress Cataloging in Publication Data

Batey, Richard A   1933-
    Thank God, I'm OK.

    Includes bibliographical references and index.
    1. Christian life—1960- 2. Transactional analysis. I. Title.
BV4501.2.B3842   248'.4   76-14358

ISBN 0-687-41389-3

Scripture quotations unless otherwise noted are from the Revised
Standard Version of the Bible, copyrighted 1946, 1952 © 1971, 1973 by
the Division of Christian Education, National Council of Churches of
Christ in the U.S.A., and are used by permission.

Scripture quotation noted RSV Apoc. is from the Revised Standard
Version Apocrypha, copyrighted © 1957.

Figures 2 and 3 contain an adaptation of "The updating function of
the Adult through reality testing," which is illustrated in *I'm
OK–You're OK* by Thomas A. Harris, M.D. Copyright © 1967, 1968,
1969 by Thomas A. Harris, M.D. Adapted by permission of Harper &
Row, Publishers, Inc., New York, and Jonathan Cape Ltd., London.
Figure 4 is adapted from *Man, the Manipulator* by Everett L.
Shostrum.

MANUFACTURED BY THE PARTHENON PRESS AT
NASHVILLE, TENNESSEE, UNITED STATES OF AMERICA

TO

Carolyn,
a free spirit

PREFACE

Some people today are living with zest and a sense of security and personal worth. They are spontaneous, affectionate, creative, and responsible. Their lives are focused on some meaning beyond themselves, and they pursue their goals with gusto. Others observe this joyful living with envy and wonder what is the secret source of this vitality. "How," they ask, "can I also tap the power of life?" For them life is characterized by anxiety, insecurity, and despair. They empathize with Paul's complaint, "Wretched man that I am! Who will deliver me from this body of death?"

The answer to the experience of alienation and lifelessness comes in the awareness that we are OK before God. "Thanks be to God through Jesus Christ our Lord" (Rom. 7:25). This book is an interpretation of the gospel message of freedom in the popular language of Transactional Analysis. It is a New Testament approach to self-realization and personal freedom that tells you how to be OK for keeps.

I wish to acknowledge my gratitude to The Garrett Foundation for its support of this project. Most of the material in this book has been presented to classes both in college and church. I am appreciative of the honest responses and helpful insights that have been gained through these valuable exchanges. Competent and amiable secretarial assistance has been provided by Mrs. Patty Byrd and Mrs. Marjorie Stoner. My wife, Carolyn, has read the manuscript and contributed numerous suggestions that have helped to point out its relevance to daily living.

Memphis, Easter 1976   *Richard A. Batey*

CONTENTS

I

The Quest for Freedom

For freedom Christ has set us free; stand fast therefore, and do not submit again to a yoke of slavery.

—*Galatians 5:1*

The Challenge of Freedom

A few summers ago my family and I camped on Lake Geneva just across from the Castle of Chillon. Earlier that day we had visited the dungeon of the castle and had seen Lord Byron's name carved in one of the massive stone pillars. In the evening I sat absorbed in the sunset and in the rosy hue that it cast over the lake and landscape. I recalled the final lines of Byron's famous poem "The Prisoner of Chillon" (1816), written about François de Bonnivard, who had borne a lengthy imprisonment for conspiring with a band of patriots to establish a free republic.

> At last men came to set me free;
> I asked not why, and reckoned not where;
> It was at length the same to me,
> Fettered or fetterless to be. . . .
>
> My very chains and I grew friends,
> So much a long communion tends
> To make us what we are:—even I
> Regained my freedom with a sigh.

It is the chain whose links are forged by habit and compromise, by guilt and fear, by negative feelings and

11

poor self-image that holds us back from a vital and useful existence. These "friendly fetters" to which we cling restrict the creative energy of our lives.

The desire for freedom is a basic drive in all of us. Would you like to open your life to the larger freedom that is potentially yours? This book is an invitation to enlarge your personal freedom by appropriating the psychotherapeutic value of the New Testament faith. It is written with two specific convictions. The first is that the New Testament contains a joyful message of liberation. The proclamation of the kingdom of God means that people can triumph over the evil powers that frustrate and destroy their lives—traditions and habit, sin and guilt, loneliness and despair, sickness and death. Paul's confidence was that "in all these things we are more than conquerors through him who loved us" (Rom. 8:37).

The second conviction is that current developments in the field of psychology offer useful categories for restating the New Testament's message of freedom. The recent past has witnessed a continuing debate between the field of religion and the rising popularity of psychology. Problems once thought of as spiritual now are considered from a psychological point of view. Behavior once judged to be sinful or immoral is explained in amoral Skinnerian terms, its cause sought in the conditioning influences of one's past. [1] The trend has been for pastoral counseling to be undertaken more and more by the professional psychologist. Karl Menninger noted in his recent book *Whatever Became of Sin?*:

Some behavior once regarded as sinful has certainly undergone reappraisal. . . . Lots of sins have disap-

peared; nevertheless, I believe there is a general senti-
ment that sin is still with us, by us, and in us—
somewhere. We are made vaguely uneasy by this
consciousness, this persistent sense of guilt, and we try to
relieve it in various ways. We project the blame on to
others, we ascribe the responsibility to a group, we offer
up scapegoat sacrifices, we perform or partake in
dumb-show rituals of penitence and atonement. There is
rarely a peccavi, but there's a feeling.[2]

Presently an increasing number of psychologists who
are confronted with their patients' "spiritual problems," that is, concerns about meaning and value in
life, are speaking in terms more compatible with
religious language. These new ways of speaking of man
and his psychological needs offer useful categories for
restating the New Testament faith. The potential for a
creative dialogue between popular psychology and
biblical theology has been recognized by the
psychologist, who realizes that both fields are concerned with authentic life. Thomas Harris has observed
that: "The early Christians met to talk about an exciting
encounter, about having met a man, named Jesus, who
walked with them, who laughed with them, who cried
with them, and whose openness and compassion for
people was a central historical example of I'M OK—
YOU'RE OK."[3]

A specific area of popular psychology that demonstrates a remarkably close affinity to biblical theology is
Transactional Analysis (T.A.). The similarity between
the understanding of the human predicament, whether
spoken of as Original Sin or "universal Not-OK-ness,"
offers helpful ways of restating biblical insights. The
New Testament's proclamation of God's grace and

acceptance is not unlike the affirmation I'm OK—You're OK that T.A. sees as the outlook of the mentally healthy person.

One of the most valuable contributions of T.A. is that it has provided a simple and precise vocabulary for describing the structure of the individual personality. This language aid provides the key for unscrambling the psychological information expressed in the specialists' jargon. T.A.'s definitions of terms are easily learned and can be readily applied to understanding our personality and interpersonal relationships. The clarity and simplicity of the language has prompted wide popular acceptance. The terminology and the insights that it expresses provide the means for restating the New Testament's message of salvation. This book will suggest a new way to express old ideas with freshness and clarity and to make helpful applications of the Christian faith to daily living. This restatement of the message of salvation in the contemporary idiom holds the promise of a renewal of the experience of well-being and happiness that enthused the first Christians.

New Testament Interpretation

New Testament interpretation is a dialogue between the first Christian writers and people in another culture. The early Christians expressed their faith in the "earthen vessel" of Koine Greek, which was spoken throughout the Hellenistic world. Every statement of the gospel is influenced by the time, geography, and language of the current culture. The New Testament itself is in large measure the result of a dialogue which took place among the first believers as they shared convictions, debated issues, or witnessed to those outside the community. The temptation to relax the tension implicit within this dialogue persists. On the one hand, the doctrines of the New Testament may be repeated in a loud voice without their being intelligible to sincere and honest persons today. On the other hand, the message may be distorted by up-to-date terms that obscure its original meaning. In striving for relevance one may reduce the expectation and significance of the gospel to that of a mirror of cultural values.

Once a useful interpretation has been made, we may cling to it beyond the time that it is meaningful or insist that it is the only adequate presentation of the gospel. Dogmatism replaces understanding and relevant meaning. Archaic data is repeated with an authoritarian tone, and the freedom of spiritual growth is stifled. We may make an idol of a theological position or method of interpretation and refuse to remain open to the larger reality of God's creativity. The Christian community must test every new spiritual impulse and theological statement to see if it is consistent with the message of God's salvation. But, to become entrenched in a theological position and refuse to move forward into the emerging new world is a rejection of the spirit of excitement and expectation that inspired the first believers.

The interpretation of the New Testament in modern times has been advanced greatly by the application of historical methods of research to the text. The historical-critical approach helps to reconstruct the setting in which the books originally were written and to understand their original purpose. Scientific historical investigation is a valid tool for rediscovering the New Testament's meaning. However, an intrinsic limitation of the historical-critical method is its concentration on the recovery of the "bare facts" of history. This emphasis distracts the critical historian from the *meaning* that was primary for the first Christians—and for Christians today.[4] The awareness of this limitation has led to the recognition that other methods of interpretation must supplement or even replace the historical-critical approach. Rudolf Bultmann, in his program of demythologizing the New Testament by restating its message in the language of existential philosophy, has offered a classic example of a reinterpretation of the New Testament into modern language.[5]

More than a decade ago I visited Bultmann at his home in the university town of Marburg, West Germany. It was a sunny June afternoon and we sat out on his patio and discussed trends in New Testament theology. In the course of our conversation I asked him what advice he would give to a young person pursuing the discipline of New Testament interpretation. His response was measured and concise. His eyes, remarkably clear for one whose eightieth birthday was only six weeks away, twinkled slightly in the waning sunlight. Then in his soft but audible German he said: "Study half of the time the works of New Testament scholars and the other half the literature of your culture." Such study provides the groundwork for the continuing conversation between Christ and culture.

The restatement of the New Testament's message of salvation in terms made popular by Transactional Analysis is a vital part of this conversation. The presupposition of this reinterpretation is that *contemporary psychological analysis of the structure and function of the self is also applicable to the understanding of first-century man*. This is not to deny that our experiences in the rapidly changing modern world are in many respects novel. It is, however, to affirm that the structure of the self in first-century man and in modern man is little changed and that insights from contemporary psychology do provide access to the experience of salvation witnessed to in the New Testament. To reject this presupposition is tantamount to affirming the irrelevance of the gospel for modern secular man!

The unwillingness or inability to express the Christian faith in contemporary language produces frustration in the younger generation, who all too often find the church irrelevant to their life-styles. Some may with a display of piety accept old doctrines that they do not understand but nevertheless expound with extreme childlike sincerity. Others reject the church with iconoclastic zeal. They cannot appropriate the form of Christian doctrine and institutional church life, so they rebel against dogmatism under the banner of honesty and truth. This book's restatement of New Testament faith in the language of Transactional Analysis can provide a meaningful conversation between older and younger generations—as well as between those inside and those outside the church. It is my hope that this interpretation will stimulate the dialogue that is intrinsic to the Christian life and will be one word in the ongoing conversation that seeks to move beyond archaic language to the rediscovery of the reality of the gospel message.

To the reader a word of caution must be offered, for

obviously the biblical writers and the modern psychologists do not share an identical perspective. The psychologist is primarily interested in understanding human behavior and the structure of the self. The biblical writer's fundamental concern is the experience of salvation and man's relation to God. These two frames of reference cannot be equated. However, to the extent that the psychologist is interested in the transcendent yearnings of man—the desire for meaning, purpose, and value—he finds himself drawn into the sphere of religion. To the extent that the biblical writer is interested in describing the *experience* of man's relation to the transcendent he becomes introspective and touches on the realm of psychology.

Our present task is to explore this point of contact in restating the New Testament faith. This is not a book in the psychology of religion that deals with religious phenomena in strictly psychological categories. Rather it is a study in New Testament theology that seeks to interpret the faith in those categories provided by contemporary psychology. Beyond this comparison we will seek practical applications of the Christian message in ways that will free the human spirit. The faith of the early Christians was inspired by a man who mediates an experience of liberation and offers the way to authentic life. The dove in the New Testament has become a symbol of the Spirit that grants peace and vitality to life. This faith is not an abstract principle or intellectual idea but rather the *experience* of life lived in the power of the Spirit. As such the Spirit is not an authority to which one sacrifices one's intellect, rather it is a power that furthers understanding and fulfills human existence. In this context we hear the words of

THE QUEST FOR FREEDOM

Jesus: "You shall know the truth and the truth shall make you free." This promise, written over the portals of many halls of learning, holds the invitation to live free in spirit and soar beyond the horizons of our present world view.

For Freedom Has Christ Set Us Free

We often think of freedom in political, economic, or spatial terms—freedom of movement, freedom from civil or religious oppression, freedom to possess property. Freedom begins, however, with the ability to clearly assess our options and choose responsibly between them. In a so-called free society a person driven by compulsion or by a desire to conform to expected patterns of behavior is not free at all. On the contrary, he often experiences a loneliness and despair that bespeaks a loss of freedom.

Freedom arises in the human spirit! One summer I taught a class of inmates in the Shelby County Jail in Memphis. The title of the course was "Man's Quest for Meaning." The jail is an antiquated facility about half a century old, greatly overcrowded, and without air conditioning. In Memphis the summer temperature ranges in the high nineties or low one hundreds day after day with an oppressive humidity. These men are in a pressure box where frustration, hate, anger, and fear erupt into violence with the slightest provocation.

Selected for the class were ten men from various tanks who comprised a cross section of the inmates. These men had been convicted of narcotics violations, armed robbery, arson, rape, homosexual sadism, and murder. In our group discussions the question was raised:

19

"What is the most important meaning for your life?" The group responded intensely: "To be free!" Passion showed in the gleam of their eyes. The meaning of life focused on the desire for freedom. Even when there was not the slightest justification for this hope, there remained the expectation that new evidence, a reversal of decision, discovery of mistrial, or some surprising act of clemency—even a jailbreak—would grant release. It was their will to freedom that gave them the courage to cope with persistent despair.

Only one inmate—a bright, talkative, and affable young man—dissented from the group opinion. He volunteered: "I have been a junkie and thief most of my life. I actually am freer in this jail than I was on the street with four thousand dollars in my pocket driving a big new car and wearing expensive clothes—but hooked on drugs." He had learned that a person's freedom is not just a matter of being "out on the street" if he is not in control of his choices. Real freedom to him meant more than just room to move around. It involved the capacity to assess the options and make meaningful decisions. Of course he wanted out of jail, but he also realized that release did not guarantee his being a really free man.

Most Americans today appear to enjoy unequaled freedom. The pluralism of American society provides us with a wide range of options. Through the development of science and technology we have pushed back the natural limitations of space and time, ignorance and disease. We have more freedom to travel, more leisure time, superior health care, better food, and greater luxuries than any people in history. Through the creation of democratic institutions we experience exceptional political liberty. Our contemporary secular society has shaken off the controls of religious institutions and the Puritan ethic. New life-styles and family patterns are emerging on the rapidly changing social scene. The effect of gaining greater independence from the controls of nature, the state, and the church has been to greatly increase the choices that are available.

One would think that the increase in our options would correspondingly enhance the degree of freedom that we enjoy. The very opposite is frequently the case, however, because we are losing the capacity to make *meaningful* choices. With more and more alternatives available, the power of discrimination becomes more important. Alvin Toffler has pointed out the frustration of confronting so many options. "Today there is a hidden conflict in our lives between the pressures of acceleration and those of novelty. One forces us to make faster decisions while the other compels us to make the hardest, most time-consuming type of decisions."[6] When the acceleration of change makes coping impossible, modern man will go into a state of shock. The demand to cope effectively with rapid change requires a centered point of reference in an individual's life—a meaning that will provide stability in dealing with the ordeal of change.

Characteristic of the present situation is a disruption of the old value system. Customary ways of thinking and reacting are no longer adequate for the rapidly changing circumstances that we confront. Many of the values by which we have lived are obsolete. At the very time when we need to make wise decisions more rapidly in order to cope with the acceleration of change, we find ourselves unable to maintain the values by

21

which we and our forefathers have lived. The increase in options when coupled with the decrease in values creates anxiety.[7] Do we not feel the pull of the maelstrom of change? Watergate has become a sobering symbol of the loss of a center of values for our nation. But, there is also the prospect of detecting a meaning for our lives that may enable us to steer a course toward a newer world.

> 'Tis not too late to seek a newer world.
> Push off, and sitting well in order smite
> The sounding furrows; for my purpose holds
> To sail beyond the sunset, and the baths
> Of all the western stars, until I die.

> Alfred Lord Tennyson "Ulysses"

Where can we find a rudder to navigate successfully the waters of Charybdis?

II
Toward Self-Understanding

*I do not understand my own actions. For I do not do what I want,
but I do the very thing I hate.*

—Romans 7:15

The ego states described by Transactional Analysis
have been detailed in a number of current books.[1] For
our purpose it will suffice to sketch the structure of the
personality and to define the basic terms used by T.A.
Then we can proceed to point out in subsequent
chapters the value of these terms for a restatement of the
New Testament's message of salvation and its implications for Christian living.

The Brain as Video Recorder

The research of the famous neurosurgeon Wilder
Penfield provided the model of the brain that was
adopted by Eric Berne, the originator of Transactional
Analysis. Penfield, a 1913 Princeton graduate and
Rhodes scholar, studied the nervous system with some
of the world's foremost experts in Britain and Germany.
It was in Germany from Dr. Otfried Foester that
Penfield learned the surgical technique that led to his
revolutionary discovery. The operation was developed
as a treatment for epilepsy resulting from brain
damage. The patient remains *fully conscious* throughout
the operation. Under local anesthetic a flap of the scalp

and the bone beneath are cut and held back with retractors. Next, the tough membrane that covers the brain, the *dura,* is opened exposing a saucer-size area of the brain.

Penfield stimulated areas of the brain, a three-pound mass of pink-gray jelly traversed by throbbing red arteries, with a mild electrical current. The brain does not have feeling and the patient does not experience pain. However, the effect of the galvanic probe could be reported by the patient. The stimulation of certain areas of the brain made an arm jump or an eye wink. Such responses had been carefully charted on a map of the cerebral cortex. During this surgical procedure in 1931 the historic breakthrough occurred.[2] The patient was a middle-aged housewife. When Penfield's electrode stimulated a point on one of the two temporal lobes above the ears, the woman exclaimed that she seemed to be having her baby all over again. She continued to describe the delivery in detail as if reliving it.

From this amazing discovery a succession of similar occurrences led to the following conclusions concerning the brain: (1) certain areas of the brain are data banks that function like a video recorder; (2) the *feelings* that accompany an experience are recorded as an inseparable part of the experience; (3) an individual is capable of existing in two states of consciousness simultaneously (the woman was able to *relive* the experience of the delivery room while at the same time describing it to others in the operating room); and (4) these recordings of experiences and the feelings locked within them can be replayed in the present. The replaying of these memory tapes has a decisive effect on present feelings, attitudes, and interpersonal relationships.[3]

Definition of Terms

Eric Berne, the father of T.A., noticed that his patients changed ego states as he observed them and listened to them. He became aware that each ego state was identifiable by a consistent pattern of behavior reflecting a correspondingly consistent pattern of feelings and experiences. Careful analysis revealed that each person has three separate and distinct ego states. These Berne labeled Parent, Adult, and Child, because of the specific source of their origin.[4] Drawing on the model of the brain as a video recorder based on Penfield's research, Berne concluded that all the experiences of childhood are stored in the brain's memory bank. These memory tapes include data the child learns uncritically from parents and other authority figures. In addition there are recordings of the feelings and distorted perceptions of the young child. We must here define briefly Parent, Adult, and Child, although more complete definitions will be given in the appropriate chapters.

The Parent

The *Parent* is a *taught* concept of life. It contains the attitudes and behavior accepted uncritically from parents and other *external authority* sources. The Parent may be recognized by behavior that is prejudicial, critical, demanding, or nurturing. Inwardly it is experienced as archaic Parent tapes that affect the inner Child. You are in your Parent ego state when you are acting, feeling, or thinking the way you recall your own parents.

25

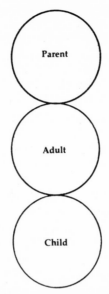

Fig. 1. The Personality

Physical clues of the Parent are: the pointing index finger, the index finger placed across the lips, horrified look, frowning, sighing, wringing hands, hands on hips, arms folded across the chest, foot tapping, patting another on the head.

Verbal clues of the Parent are words spoken thoughtlessly; they are evaluative words that are prejudicial and closed to present reality. "Should" and "ought" as well as "always" and "never" may reveal the Parent state. Other words frequently expressing an archaic Parent response are: "stupid," "shocking," "disgusting," "ridiculous," "absurd," "naughty," and "poor dear."

TOWARD SELF-UNDERSTANDING

The Child

The *Child* is a *felt* concept of life. It contains all those impulses that are natural to infants. Whenever you feel or act like you did when you were a child, you are in your Child ego state. There are three aspects to the Child ego state—the Natural Child, the Adapted Child, and the Little Professor.[5] The *Natural Child* is affectionate, impulsive, sensuous, uncensored, and curious. It is also fearful, self-indulgent, self-centered, rebellious, and aggressive. Many of these natural impulses, if undisciplined, may prove dangerous to the infant or unacceptable to society. The infant must be trained to behave safely and acceptably. Since he is totally dependent on others, he has no choice but to conform to the behavior demanded. The *Adapted Child* is that part of the Child ego state that is primarily influenced by parents. It is manifest in common patterns of adaptation such as complying, withdrawing, and procrastinating. The inevitable consequence of this civilizing process is that every child assumes the position I'm Not OK—You're OK. This is a feeling derived from the very situation of infantile dependency and is a universal human experience. The third part of the Child ego state is the *Little Professor*. It is innately intuitive, creative, and manipulative.

Physical clues of the Child ego state are: Natural Child—hugging, kissing, laughing, giggling, squirming, teasing, hitting, nose thumbing; Adapted Child—pouting, temper tantrums, hiding, downcast eyes, whining voice, shrugging shoulders; Little Professor—touching, smelling, looking, opening, pulling, stacking, smiling.

Verbal clues that help to identify the Child are "baby talk" and expressions such as: I want, I wish, I guess, when I grow up, bigger, biggest, better, best. More characteristic of the Little Professor are the interrogatives: how, who, when, where, why, and what.

The Adult

The *Adult* ego state is a *thought* concept of life. The Adult functions like a computer to collect and organize factual data, to compute options, and to estimate probabilities. It is objective, dispassionate, and oriented toward the understanding of present reality. You are in your Adult ego state when you are objectively gathering and analyzing factual data and calculating probabilities. The Adult also has the capacity to test the content of the Parent and feelings of the Child to find out if they are consistent with reality.

Physical clues of the Adult are those facial expressions characteristic of an attentive, curious, and thoughtful person—intense gaze, eyes blinking, head nodding in understanding, quizzical expression seeking clarification.

Verbal clues of the Adult in addition to the interrogatives of the Little Professor—which is the Adult beginning to function in the little person—are analytical and comparative terms such as: in what way, how much, unknown, possible, probable, false, true, objective, subjective, I think, it is my opinion, and I see.

Script Analysis

The accumulation of clinical experience indicates that between the ages of three and seven a child develops a

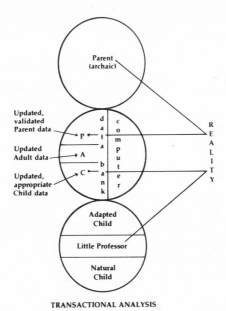

TRANSACTIONAL ANALYSIS

Fig. 2. The Updating Function of the Adult
Through Reality Testing

"dramatic script" for his life.[6] This psychological script
is similar to a theatrical script, with a plot, a cast of
characters, acts and scenes, climax, and final curtain.
Later the elements of the life script will be compulsively
acted out on the stage of life. Transactions between the
little person and parent figures serve to program script
instructions into the Child ego state. Scripting begins
with the nonverbal messages expressed by touch, voice
quality, and facial expressions. The message received
by an infant held and stroked affectionately will be
quite different from that received by the infant who is

handled roughly or left to cry in his crib. From these messages the child constructs a script about how he will live his life. He learns to play specific roles in this drama—victim, persecutor, rescuer—and unconsciously seeks others to fill out the corresponding cast of characters. The method of detecting these early unconscious decisions as to how life will be lived is Script Analysis.

The script transmitted from parents to their children may be passed on within the family from generation to generation. Family scripts program the children with the life-style and attitudes they will have. These family scripts differ widely among families that are royal, wealthy, poor, educated, illiterate, devoutly religious, or professionally oriented.

Cultural scripts also are transferred from one generation to the next. These cultural scripts are visible in the national character of a people. The script of the Germans is distinctly different from that of the French. The Italians and the English have their own unique national qualities. The American life-style is markedly different from Communist China's.

Scripting results from the messages that we received from our family and culture and the unconscious decisions that we make concerning these messages. While our script will determine how we view our life and how we relate to others, we are not permanently bound by our original script. We may make new conscious decisions about our script based on new evidence and experience, just as a playwright reworks the script of his play in the light of audience reaction and a better understanding of the interaction between his characters. This re-editing may prove difficult and at times disturbing, but it can lead to a freer, more creative, and happier life drama.

The New Testament's portrayal of the life of Jesus is not motivated by the mere desire to produce a factual biography of an outstanding man. Jesus is dramatically presented as the Son of God, whose ministry and message redefine the nature of authentic life and thereby provide the script for a new life-style—a new humanity. Paul, for example, found his life rescripted by the acceptance of Jesus as his Lord and declared: "I have been crucified with Christ; it is no longer I who live, but Christ who lives in me; and the life I now live in the flesh I live by faith in the Son of God, who loved me and gave himself for me" (Gal. 2:20). But, what is the nature of this freedom? How may I appropriate it to my day-to-day living?

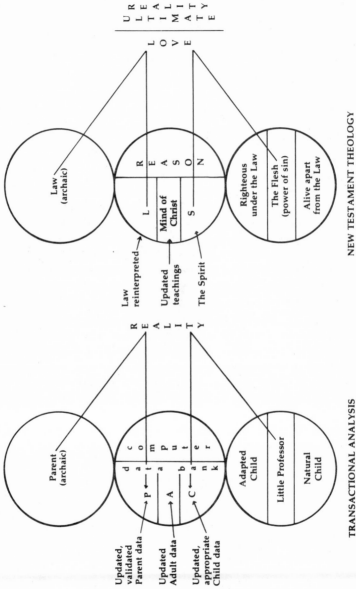

TRANSACTIONAL ANALYSIS   NEW TESTAMENT THEOLOGY

Fig. 3.   Comparative Diagrams

III
Sin and Not-OK-ness

All have sinned and fall short of the glory of God.

"What's wrong with me anyway?"

Recently I asked a class of thirty-five college students discussing the search for personal values in contemporary society how often each used the word "sin" during an average week. It was somewhat surprising to learn that only five students used "sin" in normal conversation. Four of the five pointed out that when they did say "sin," it was understood as being in quotes as though expressing an archaic concept from their parents or clergy. Only one stated that "sin" was a meaningful and useful term in his vocabulary. This sampling could be repeated with similar results across the nation. However, this situation in a church-related liberal arts college in the heart of the Bible Belt, where most students have been exposed to traditional views of American religion, underscores the need for a new look at the meaning of "sin."

The virtual disappearance of the word "sin" from young people's conversations today does not necessarily signify a lack of sensitivity to moral values. Many young people are more keenly concerned with moral values than are their parents. But, there is a growing unwillingness to repeat traditional language and to

33

follow moral codes that seem irrelevant to life decisions. New ways of talking about the experience of "sin" are current in language that reveals alienation. One frequently hears the expressions: "exploiting or using someone," "failing to be responsible," "putting somebody down," "being thoughtless, insensitive, or selfish" or just "feeling alone, worthless, and depressed" to articulate the experience customarily expressed by the word "sin."

The Source of Not-OK-ness

Transactional Analysis has provided us with some helpful insights into our behavior and offers the prospect for a new understanding of sin in the New Testament. *Both T.A. and the New Testament are in basic agreement that man's predicament is rooted in the experience of alienation from the source of his life.* T.A. traces this Not-OK-ness to the feelings recorded in every infant during the trauma of birth. The New Testament traces the experience of alienation shared by all men to the Fall of Adam and his expulsion from Paradise. T.A. and the New Testament concur that our primary problem is the condition of estrangement, and both offer comparable solutions to our plight. First we will examine T.A.'s analysis of our Not-OK-ness, and then we will take a fresh look at the New Testament's understanding of sin.

What is the origin of our Not OK feelings? Clinical research with infants has revealed that as a result of the trauma of birth Not OK feelings are indelibly recorded on the brain of each infant. But, how does this happen? Let us consider the trauma of birth.

As the fetus develops, it floats in a liquid with a constant temperature; it is protected from extremes of light and sound. The unborn infant is very sensitive. If a woman more than six months pregnant is exposed to the sunlight, the fetus will see the light as a golden glow. The fetus can hear its mother's joints crack, her intestines rumble, and the steady and rhythmic beat of her heart. The symbiotic union of mother and infant provides the unborn baby with the oxygen and nourishment necessary for its growth.[1]

Gradually as the infant grows, the former spaciousness of the womb seems to close tighter and tighter about him. He has outgrown his ideal environment and feels the womb as a prison restricting movement and life. Then the prison comes alive and begins to assault, stifle, and crush the infant. Dr. Frederick Leboyer, who has delivered more than 10,000 babies, dramatically describes the infant's experience of birth in the best selling book *Birth Without Violence*.

> The infant is like one possessed. Mad with agony and misery, alone, abandoned, it fights with the strength of despair. The monster drives the baby lower still. And not satisfied with crushing, it twists it in a refinement of cruelty. The infant's head and body execute a corkscrew motion to clear the narrow passage of the pelvis.[2]

Birth in one respect is freedom, but in another respect it is separation and isolation within the great abyss.

> Then that everything explodes! The whole world bursts open. No more tunnel, no prison, no monster. The child is born. And the barrier . . . ? Disappeared, thrown away. Nothing!—except the void, with all its horror.

Freedom!—and it is intolerable. Where am I . . . ?
Everything was pressing in on me, crushing me, but at
least I had a form. My mother, my hated prison—where
are you? Alone, I am nothingness, dizziness. Take me
back! Contain me again. Destroy me! But let me exist.[3]

Within moments the umbilical cord is cut, severing
the tie binding the baby to the only world he has
known. Then he is taken by the heels and held aloft, his
spine suddenly pulled straight. He feels the sharp pain
of the doctor's slap on the tender skin that has only felt
the warm velvet of the womb. He gasps in pain as he
draws the first breath of burning oxygen into his
sensitive lungs. The eyes that have been protected from
light now are blinded by the white brightness of the
delivery room. Delicate ears hear the sharp and loud
sounds to which older ears are accustomed. But, more
than this blend of pains is the terrifying experience of
separation, isolation, and helplessness.

This experience of pain, isolation, and complete
dependence is recorded in the newborn's brain as Not
OK feelings. These feelings are obviously prerational
and preverbal, yet they are *permanent in every infant*. If
the mother or an attendant did not come and rescue the
baby, it would soon die. The need for nourishment and
physical stroking is essential for the baby's survival. If
the physical stroking that is present in normal infant
care is withheld, the baby will waste away and die—a
condition known as marasmus.

> Spitz has found that infants deprived of handling over a
> long period will tend at length to sink into an irreversible
> decline and are prone to succumb eventually to intercur-
> rent disease. In effect, this means that what he calls
> emotional deprivation can have a fatal outcome.[4]

The positive support necessary for the infant's survival leads inevitably to the emotional position I'm Not OK—You're OK. Alone I am separated, helpless, cold, hungry, and suffering. You come with food, warmth, a clean diaper, and affection. This initial emotional position assumed by every infant is its first attempt to gain a state of equilibrium in the contingencies and uncertainty of his existence. The security of the womb is replaced by an emotional position that assumes something solid and predictable in life. The I'm Not OK—You're OK position is the first glimmer of the Adult in the little person, i.e., the Little Professor, attempting to make "intellectual elaborations on the construct of causality."[5] This position is permanently recorded in the infant during the first year and will influence his every action.

A baby soon discovers that certain random actions on his part are met with predictable results. Cries of pain from hunger or gas bring mother to his crib with a feeding or comfort. She picks him up and cares for him and he feels the security of her warm breast and her gentle hand touching his back. He quickly learns to manipulate others to relieve the burden of his Not-OK-ness. With time he refines his skill. These manipulations spring from the feelings of Not-OK-ness and are basically selfish efforts to survive and obtain comfort and security. These maneuvers are the beginning of "games" that selfishly manipulate others for "payoffs."

The I'm Not OK—You're OK position that is assumed during the first year may be changed to one of two other emotional positions during the second or third year. The *abandoned child,* who after he is old enough to walk virtually ceases to be stroked, may conclude I'm Not

OK—You're Not OK, because the source of his OK-ness has been withdrawn. The *battered child* on the other hand feels better off when alone than when subjected to the pain and abuse of a frustrated or sadistic parent. This child may take the emotional position I'm OK—You're Not OK. The change from the first emotional position to a second position is permanent. People do not shift back and forth between positions.

The Power of Sin

T.A.'s awareness that Not OK feelings are indelibly recorded in the brain of every child and are the cause of selfish behavior helps us to understand the nature of sin as described in the New Testament. For Paul, sin is not simply unacceptable behavior but a power controlling his actions. Sin is a condition of being. It springs from man's *state of estrangement* from the source of life—God the Creator. Paul analyzes how this "Not-OK-ness" operates in his own life. "Now if I do what I do not want, it is no longer I that do it, but sin which dwells within me" (Rom. 7:20). Sin is a power for Paul rooted deeply in his psyche and controlling his conduct. The authentic life from which he felt separated was impossible to achieve because efforts to obtain true life were selfishly motivated. "We know that the law is spiritual; but I am carnal, sold under sin. I do not understand my own actions. For I do not do what I want, but I do the very thing I hate" (Rom. 7:14-15).

Paul also observed the power of sin at work in others—both Jew and Greek. "For there is no distinction; since all have sinned and fall short of the glory of God" (Rom. 3:22*b*-23). It was quite natural for Paul to move from psychological insights to theological conclusions. His anthropology is worked out in terms of man's relation to powers, both demonic and beneficent, influencing him. Bultmann has correctly pointed out that for Paul "every assertion about God is simultaneously an assertion about man and vice versa."[6] The human experience of alienation acquires for Paul theological dimensions.

What then is the human condition as Paul sees it? First, man is a creature dependent and unable to secure true life by himself. Man's condition as creature corresponds to the situation of a newborn infant who *feels his absolute dependence* when separated from the womb. For Paul, man's condition as creature is not evil. However, man's awareness that he is separated from the source of life presents him with a fundamental alternative. Will the power of life be found by trusting in himself or by opening to the power of life beyond? *Not OK feelings are present in every person and are not to be equated with sin. Not-OK-ness is the feeling of creaturely dependence. Sin is trusting in one's own ability to attain life.* Self-trust is *hamartia*, "missing the mark," of trusting in God, the goal and fulfillment of existence. The conduct produced by trusting in one's own efforts to secure life is, in effect, slavery to sin.

Paul describes in Romans 1:18-31 the condition of man under the wrath of God. The Creator reveals himself through the creation. "Ever since the creation of the world his invisible nature, namely, his eternal power and deity, has been clearly perceived in the things that have been made" (Rom. 1:20). But, man refuses to recognize God and seeks within creation for the fulfillment of life. God responds by leaving man in the world in which God's presence is not acknowledged. The eclipse of God is seen in Paul's statement that "the wrath of God is revealed from heaven against all ungodliness and wickedness of men who by their wickedness suppress the truth" (Rom. 1:18).

Man's predicament is that his awareness of creaturely dependence leads to self-trust rather than trust in God. The result is alienation instead of reconciliation. "For I have already charged that all men, both Jews and Greeks, are under the power of sin" (Rom. 3:9). Paul supports this indictment with proof texts from the Old Testament: "None is righteous, no, not one; no one understands, no one seeks for God" (Rom. 3:10b-11). "All have turned aside, together they have gone wrong; no one does good, not even one" (Rom. 3:12). The power of sin controls man's actions and causes the loss of his freedom.

The Yahwist's story of Adam's Fall related in Genesis 3 provided Paul with the script for understanding man. As a boy reared in a strict Pharisaical home, the narrative of the first man would have been among Paul's earliest memories. This story influenced his perception of human nature. It was quite natural for Paul to express the alienation that he observed in all men in terms of Adam, the archetypal man. He attributes to Adam the qualities characteristic of all men. The Greeks could readily speak of the essential nature of man in philosophical abstractions, but Paul found the Old Testament imagery more familiar in describing human nature. "Therefore as sin came into the world through one man and death through sin, . . . so death spread to all men because all men sinned" (Rom. 5:12; cf. I Cor. 15:20-23). This type of language was current for Paul's Jewish contemporaries. Toward the end of the first century a Palestinian Jew wrote: "O Adam, what have you done? For though it was you who sinned, the fall was not yours alone, but ours also who are your descendants. For what good is it to us, if an eternal age has been promised to us, but we have done deeds that bring death?" (II Esdras 7:48-49 RSV Apoc.).

The Yahwist's narrative furnishes the backdrop for Paul's teaching concerning the origin and nature of sin. The Lord God made man from the dust of the ground and breathed into him the breath of life. Man in the womb of paradise was at peace with nature, himself, and God. But, Adam and Eve desired to be like God and succumbed to the serpent's temptation to eat of the fruit that God had forbidden. They attempted to assert their independence from their Creator. Becoming aware of their nakedness, they hid from God, only to be discovered and driven from the Garden of Eden. An angel with a flaming sword guarded the gate and prevented their return to paradise and their access to the tree of life. Now man was subject to the experience of alienation from God (the source of his life) as well as from nature and his companion. Death reminds man that the power of life is not within himself.

An interesting sidelight to our comparison is seen in the belief of the Greeks from the time of Hippocrates that babies provide the stimulus that begins labor. Contrary to the widely accepted belief today that babies are passive at their birth, the infant actually does begin to struggle in order to free itself from the prison of the womb and initiates labor just as the ancients thought. Adam also rebelled against the limitations imposed by paradise and so energized the Force that expelled him.[7]

In the Gospel of John, darkness is the major symbol expressing man's alienation. The world of mankind is imprisoned in darkness because men fail to recognize that their life is dependent on God. All things have been made through the divine Word who was in the beginning with God. "In him was life, and the life was the light of men" (John 1:4). This light shines in the darkness, and so, knowledge of the source of all life is available. But men shut their eyes against the light. They look within themselves for the power to live. This blindness causes man's condition of alienation. When "the true light that enlightens every man" comes into the world that he has made, men neither recognize nor receive the light; they prefer to remain in darkness.

In the Fourth Gospel the Jewish leaders are singled out as the epitome of blindness because they are arrogant and self-righteous. They are like blind teachers holding up unlit torches; for they do not see that they enlighten no one. "Darkness is nothing other than shutting one's self up against the light. It is turning away from the origin of one's existence, away from that which alone offers the possibility of illumining one's existence." [8] Blindness then is looking within one's self for true life. Walking in darkness, vainly imagining that life is within one's own control, is life alienated from the light of God's love.

In the spring of 1974 my wife, Carolyn, and I traveled to Rome with my class studying the Italian Renaissance. I revisited the Sistine Chapel and gazed for a long time at Michelangelo's frescoes adorning the ceiling. As I asked what was the universal appeal of this masterpiece, my eyes were drawn to two of the center panels. One depicts Adam's relaxed body with his outstretched hand receiving the gift of life from his Maker. The other portrays the expulsion of Adam and Eve from Paradise with their posture revealing their shame and fear. These two panels seem to capture and convey the essence of human existence to which we each answer, "Yes." Here the special genius of the Hebrew sage and the Renaissance master meld like the paint and plaster of these frescoes. We are created for and seek for true life and self-fulfillment, but we also are threatened by the fundamental awareness of alienation from the source of life. This is the basic dilemma with which we must contend in the quest for a healthy, happy, and productive life. If alienation is a universal and indelible experience, how does it influence my behavior? How can I free myself from its control?

IV
The Little Professor

When I was a child, I spoke like a child, I thought like a child, I reasoned like a child.

—I Corinthians 13:11

We have observed that every newborn infant's experience of isolation and dependency is recorded as Not OK feelings. If it were not for the adults who care for the child, satisfying his food-hunger and stimulation-hunger, he would soon die from apathy. These positive strokes are necessary for survival and lead inevitably to the emotional position I'm Not OK—You're OK. The infant's basic drive for survival causes him to seek positive strokes in order to relieve his Not OK feelings. His overriding concern is to get OK people to give him, a Not OK person, the necessary positive strokes.

The Art of Manipulation

The infant quickly learns to manipulate his world for self-satisfaction. He associates certain random actions with a somewhat predictable response. "Every child, even without acting lessons, discovers at an early age how to manipulate people and things. Almost every infant has to figure out how to bring someone to his side. Often by trial and error, he finds that if he pretends to be frightened or ill, mother will come running to his crib."[1] The child screaming in the dark at 2:00 A.M. can cause marvelous things to happen. Lights come on. Mother lifts him from the bed, rocks, changes, and feeds him before returning him to a soft warm blanket. The infant soon learns to refine his magic. Everett Shostrom points out that these initial manipulations lead to bigger games. "Thus the toddling infant soon learns to drool or coo on cue, or have a temper tantrum to get what he wants. His environment thereafter provides constant schooling and ample encouragement in the arts of manipulation."[2]

As the child grows older the need for stroking remains, but the close physical contact with the mother grows less. Through a process of compromises, or sublimation, stimulus-hunger is transformed into what Eric Berne calls recognition-hunger.[3] The child learns to substitute more subtle and symbolic forms of handling for diminishing physical contact. Efforts to gain recognition, and so relieve the Not OK feelings, become more individual and form a recurring pattern of interpersonal relationships. The Little Professor, i.e., the emerging Adult in the little person, becomes increasingly skilled at manipulating others for a positive stroke, a "payoff." These manipulations are *games!* Berne has given this popular definition: "A game is an ongoing series of complementary ulterior transactions progressing to a well-defined, predictable outcome. Descriptively it is a recurring set of transactions, often repetitious, superficially plausible, with a concealed motivation; or, more colloquially, a series of moves with a snare, or 'gimmick.'"[4]

One key word in the definition of games is "ulterior." What appears on the surface to be taking place is not what is really happening. The manipulator hides his true feelings and purpose behind a facade in order to prevent the detection of his real intentions. He is a poker player whose face conceals the cards in his hand. He is a con artist who disguises the "hook" until his victim feels the "sting." He is the salesman replacing people with profits, the politician concentrating on image instead of honesty, the Pharisee substituting religious form for faithfulness. The intrinsic character of games is that they are deceptions calculated to manipulate others for personal advantage. Berne distinguishes the game from other kinds of activities. "Procedures may be successful, rituals effective, and pastimes profitable, but all of them are by definition candid. . . . Every game, on the other hand, is basically dishonest, and the outcome has a dramatic, as distinct from merely exciting, quality." [5]

Continual attempts to manipulate others in order to relieve Not-OK-ness prevents the achievement of openness and genuine intimacy. The result is that we are forced more and more into isolation and find real communication more difficult. Inevitably we feel the great estrangement or separation that the New Testament calls "missing the mark" or sin.

The manipulator also loses touch with his inner feelings. He is so caught up in a calculating and exploitative pattern of behavior that he becomes insensitive to his own desires. He experiences a loss of vitality and motivation—a lack of joy and zest for living. On the surface he may appear quite successful, as a result of his skillful manipulation of others, but his heart is not in his work or recreation. The bland professional smile, programmed movements, stereotyped response betray the loss of spontaneity. He envies those who are living their lives with inner direction and lip-smacking gusto.

Ironically, losing touch with his own real feelings and desires makes the manipulator more vulnerable to the manipulations of others, because he finds it increasingly difficult to respond with honesty and originality to their ploys. Leo Tolstoy brilliantly described the accomplished bureaucrat who achieved success by manipulation and conformity. Ivan Ilych lies on his death bed reviewing the meaning of his life and thinks: "There is one bright spot there at the back, at the beginning of life, and afterwards all becomes blacker and blacker and proceeds more and more rapidly—in inverse ratio to the square of the distance from death." [6]

Our modern culture has emphasized scientific and technological control of nature and man as well. We have stressed production and consumption until the average office employee and assembly line worker produce what they do not understand and, in turn, consume what they do not need. Erich Fromm continues to warn that our marketplace mentality endangers the essential nature of man. He sees as the specter of mechanized society a megamachine "devoted to maximal material output and consumption, directed by computers; and in this social process, man himself is being transformed into a part of the total machine, well fed and entertained, yet passive, unalive, and with little feeling." [7] In the words of T. S. Eliot, we are the "hollow men." Manipulated by a materialistic and capitalistic script, we are yet undesirous of freeing ourselves from its power. No other system has created more "willing slaves" than has capitalism. But, what are the wages of our thralldom in terms of the quality of our life?

It may be helpful before turning to the New Testament's understanding of sin to look at the basic patterns of manipulation that are at work in our society. After all, we are all manipulators some of the time, and frequently someone else is attempting to manipulate us. Everett Shostrom has analyzed the patterns of manipulation in which we are involved.[8] Frederick Perls, the founder of Gestalt therapy, was Dr. Shostrom's therapist and teacher and significantly influenced his work. Shostrom has detected eight fundamental kinds of manipulation that result from exaggerating specific characteristics. He links each type with its polar opposite to make four pairs.

1. The *Dictator* intimidates others by his strength. He dominates others with orders and authority. Types of the Dictator are: the Boss, the Rank Puller, and the Bureaucratic Administrator.

2. The *Weakling* is the direct opposite of the Dictator, controlling by exaggerated sensitivity. The Weakling is the Worrier, the Confused One, the Withdrawer, and the Giver-Upper.

3. The *Calculator* controls by outwitting others. He is the Con Artist, the Blackmailer, the High Pressure Salesman, the Seducer, the Intellectualizor.

4. The opposite of the Calculator is the *Clinging Vine*, who manipulates by exaggerated dependency. He enjoys being cared for. He is the Parasite, the Hypochondriac, the Attention Demander, the Helpless One.

5. The *Bully* controls by aggression and threats. He is the Tough Guy, the Humiliator, or the Hater. The female equivalent is the Bitch or Nagger.

6. The *Nice Guy* overemphasizes his love and caring. He is nonassuming and helpful to a fault. He kills with

kindness. Variations of the Nice Guy are the Virtuous One, the Pleaser, the Noninvolved One, the Nonviolent One, the Conformist.

7. The *Judge* is excessively critical. He is concerned to place blame and point out fault. He is resentful and slow to forgive. Types of the Judge are the Know-It-All, the Comparer, and the Convictor.

8. The polar opposite of the Judge is the *Protector.* He is so protective of others that their own sense of responsibility and independence is weakened. He is the Defender, the Mother Hen, the Martyr, the Unselfish One, the Helper.

Fig. 4. The Manipulative Types

Manipulations are the games motivated by Not OK feelings that we play for self-serving ends. Individual games combine to form a life-style, a script determining how we relate to others. Our behavior becomes controlled by our pseudophilosophy of life until we experience more keenly our alienation. Amy Harris in the chapter "P-A-C and Moral Values" that she contributed to her husband's book *I'm OK—You're OK* grasps the theological implication of T.A.'s understanding of the human predicament—Not-OK-ness. "This [feeling of Not-OK-ness] is a tragedy, but it does not become demonstrable evil until the first game is begun, the first ulterior move is made toward another person to ease the burden of the Not OK. This first retaliatory effort demonstrates . . . intrinsic badness'—or original sin—from which [a person] is told he must repent."[9] The more we try to overcome the experience of alienation, the more deceptive become our actions, and the more estrangement dominates our lives.

Life in the Flesh

The New Testament writers point out that man's experience of alienation leads to egocentric manipulations. Paul is especially helpful for our understanding of the dynamics of sin. Man trusting in his own ability to secure OK-ness or the promise of life attempts to exploit his fellow man and even God. Paul refers to the life of self-trust as life in the flesh. Fleshly existence means refusing to acknowledge one's creaturely dependence on God and seeking within one's own resources for the fulfillment of life. Paul observes three basic manifestations of man's sinful condition: social sins, idolatry, and legalism. The first results from efforts to manipulate others from a Not OK position, and the last two are attempts to manipulate deity.

For Paul, idolatry expresses man's sinfulness because it is man's attempt to control God by ritual and sacrifice. Idolatry is a refusal to acknowledge God's sovereignty over all of life. Paul points out that knowledge of God is possible for man through awareness of creation, that is, awareness of God's "eternal power and deity" (Rom. 1:20). But man resists trusting his life to that power he detects within creation. Man seeking to control his own life and destiny exchanges "the glory of the immortal God for images resembling mortal man or birds or animals or reptiles" (Rom. 1:23). The idolater exchanges the truth that God is the source and destiny of human existence for the lie that man is the master of his own fate. The false belief that man can secure life when joined to the experience of alienation, leads to various attempts to manipulate deity. The making of graven images and performance of pagan rituals, sacrificial rites, and priestly shows are all efforts to influence the gods to bestow a blessing or at least to avert a disaster. *Idolatrous worship arises from the misconception that the Creator can be manipulated in the same way as something within creation.*

Once man thinks of himself as having the power to manipulate God for selfish advantage, his whole perception is distorted. Paul says of men that "their senseless minds were darkened." Man does not seek the truth with intellectual honesty and integrity, but uses his reason, i.e., the Little Professor, to rationalize his desires and implement his schemes. Paul shared the Jewish aversion to idolatry—especially condemned by the prophet Isaiah from whom Paul quotes in Romans 3:15-17. But, the apostle knew that iconoclastic methods could not cure the basic problem of self-trust.

The Gospel of John also depicts man's basic condition as being separated from the source of life. In the prologue of the Gospel, the author states that the creative Word, the Logos through whom all things have been made, has within him the power of life. The source of life is expressed through the symbol of light. There are two ways open to man: (1) to walk in the light and thus be open to the source of life, i.e., to have faith in the Logos and trust in love; or (2) to walk in the darkness and thus trust in one's own ability to achieve life. When the light of love appeared in the world through the person of Jesus, men closed themselves to its power (John 1:9-11). "And this is the judgment, that the light has come into the world, and men loved darkness rather than light, because their deeds were evil" (John 3:19). The resulting blindness is characteristic of even the Pharisees, the so-called best of men, who expected by their self-righteousness to obtain life (John 9:40-41). Darkness is therefore an expression of man's basic separation from true life with God. Walking in darkness leads to deeds that are hateful and destructive of community. The basic experience of Not-OK-ness leads inevitably to the perversion of interpersonal relationships. For "he who hates his brother is in the darkness . . . and does not know where he is going, because the darkness has blinded his eyes" (I John 2:11).

Paul maintains that man's rejection of God's sovereign love results in a society that reveals the wrath of God. Each person seeks to secure his life against the threat and exploitations of others. Karl Barth's comment is especially lucid: "The enterprise of setting up the 'No-God' is avenged by its success." [10] Each man turns on his fellow and exploits him for some payoff. Games played with an ulterior motive do not relieve the experience of Not-OK-ness, but rather increase the sense of loneliness and isolation. The Not OK feelings that control our relations with others produce manipulations. We trust in our own efforts to gain true life or OK-ness. Turning inward in search of life's fulfillment causes us to close out God, the power of life beyond. Self-trust and the sinful deeds that it causes are what Paul describes as "life in the flesh." "To set the mind on the flesh is death" because trusting in self we miss the mark of having faith in God. "For the mind that is set on the flesh is hostile to God; it does not submit to God's law, indeed it cannot; and those who are in the flesh cannot please God" (Rom. 8:7-8). *In the language of T.A., life in the flesh is the Little Professor motivated by Not OK feelings to exploit others.*

The kinds of behavior that Paul describes as "works of the flesh" are "immorality, impurity, licentiousness, idolatry, sorcery, enmity, strife, jealousy, anger, selfishness, dissension, party spirit, envy, drunkenness, carousing, and the like" (Gal. 5:19-20a). This list is paralleled by some of Berne's games that people play. There are the Life Games of: "Alcoholic," "Kick Me," "Now I'll Get You," "See What You Made Me Do," and "Mine Is Better Than Your's." To these can be added the Sexual Games of "Let's You and Him Fight," "Perversion," "Rapo," "The Stocking Game," and "Uproar." No matter what you call it, the game is the same. In Romans 1:26-31 Paul adds more vices to his list and concludes "that those who do such things deserve to die." Indeed they are already dead, for their behavior reveals their separation from life and their experience of Not-OK-ness.

Paul's third manifestation of sin is religious legalism. This is a subtle expression of sin because on the surface this game is disguised with piety and good works. How do our efforts to do what we *ought* to do become expressions of sin?

V
The Law as Parent

I was once alive apart from the law, but when the commandment came, sin revived and I died.

—*Romans 7:9*

There is a reason why "being good" by conforming to law is so wearisome. Religious legalism results from man's effort to overcome his Not-OK-ness through conformity to religious authority, customarily expressed in the form of law. *For the legalist the law is a taught concept of life accepted uncritically; it supplies the content of his Parent*. Obedience to the law presumedly gains OK-ness, i.e., justification before God. The legalist believes that compliance with the law will manipulate God to bestow salvation. The motivation for obedience is basically selfish. Conformity to the dictates of the law, i.e., good works, supposedly will achieve the promise of life—OK-ness before God.

The Parent Ego State

The basic script of legalism is: If you obey the commandments, then you will be justified.[1] When you, a Not OK person, have done what the law requires, then you will obtain God's acceptance and salvation. *Then* you will be OK! However, the consequence of this legalistic script is to increase the experience of Not-OK-ness. When I have obeyed all the laws that I can, there are yet others to be kept. When I have discharged my duty, my duty remains to be performed again. Obedience does not remove the obligation to keep the commands in the future. Legalism becomes a treadmill continuously requiring obedience by holding forth the false promise of OK-ness. The desire for OK-ness based on our own ability to "be good" leads inevitably to despair because the script is based on the primary feelings of Not-OK-ness. Conformity to religious authority does not produce a sense of well-being. The legalist shares the futility of Sisyphus, the crafty and avaricious king of Corinth, who was condemned in Hades to push a large stone up a hill, only to have it roll back again.

Why do my most conscientious efforts to be what I *ought* to be leave me in such despair? The answer to this question lies in understanding the function of the law as Parent. The Parent ego state is composed of all the recordings in the brain that are received from external and unquestioned authority.[2] Most of this data is recorded during the first five years of a child's life and comes from the child's own parents. Since the child's critical faculties, the Adult, have not developed appreciably, he cannot examine, criticize, or evaluate this information. It is indelibly recorded as truth because it comes from the authority on which his life is dependent.

The Parent contains different types of recorded and unedited data. All the "how to" information derived from observing the behavior of parents is stored in the child's Parent ego state. For the most part this is useful data dealing with basic problems of family living—how to dress myself, tie my shoe, brush my teeth, eat soup, feed the chickens, curse the cat, smoke a cigarette, catch a butterfly, make a bed, greet a friend. In addition the Parent contains the laws and rules that govern social behavior. These rules are expressed by the thousands of "dos" and "don'ts" that a child hears: don't touch the stove, don't throw your food, don't talk with your mouth full, don't hit your sister, don't stick hairpins in the electrical outlet, don't play in the street, pick up your toys, keep your coat buttoned, play nicely with your little brother, be kind to your puppy, smile for Aunt Mable. The Parent also contains the preverbal parental communications that constitute a taught concept of life—the smiles and coos of a pleased mother, the deep jovial laughter of a proud father. Along with these reactions of delight are recorded the mother's shrill cry of alarm and the father's angry roughness.

As the child grows older and his Adult ego state develops, he acquires the capacity to reason and begins to evaluate the content of his Parent tapes. If the data in the Parent that was originally recorded as truth proves accurate and reliable, the child becomes more secure and more open to reality. The child may discover that some once valid information, with the passing of time and circumstance, has become obsolete and irrelevant to his present situation. This outdated information must then be revised or discarded. As the Adult becomes stronger, the growing child will improve in his ability to evaluate the content of his Parent, as well as to analyze and evaluate new data.

When Parent information has been reinforced with threats, physical blows, or stern behavior, the child later in life may find it emotionally disturbing to evaluate this information. Along with specific demands the helpless child records: "If you tell a lie, your nose will grow long;" "Do that again and I'll beat you black and blue;" "Do what I tell you or the bogy man will get you;" and "Be good or you will go to hell." Parent data recorded "straight," unedited and simultaneous with such threats, may accelerate a child's conformity, but it will also retard the development of his own Adult.

As a young person matures and begins to evaluate Parent data recorded in association with threats, he will frequently experience emotional disturbance or Not-OK Child feelings. He will find it easier to continue conforming to these Parent tapes than to cope with the negative feelings and guilt produced by criticizing the content of his Parent. The Parent contamination of the Adult reason produces statements and behavior that are prejudiced and archaic. This failure to update a taught concept of life portends a sacrifice of intellect and slavish following of outdated authority. Thus contamination of the Adult results in the failure to achieve wholeness. It is blindness to the truth.

The Adapted Child is the part of the Child ego state that corresponds to the Parent ego state.[3] The spontaneous and uncensored Natural Child produces behavior that is both cruel and affectionate. As a young person internalizes his parents' demands into his own Parent ego state, the Natural Child adapts to the Parent. This process of civilization or socialization produces conformity to acceptable standards of conduct. Much of this adaptation is necessary for the child's welfare and safety, as well as for the welfare and safety of others. But, the process of conformity that occurs as the Adapted Child develops causes a loss of spontaneity and vitality. The behavior of the Adapted Child is

We evaluate "Parent data" w/ our "Adult" state when it finally develops!

complying, withdrawing, and procrastinating. Shake-
speare portrayed this posture in these lines from *As You
Like It.*

> And then the whining school-boy with his satchel
> And shining morning face, creeping like snail,
> Unwillingly to school.

> [act II, scene 7, lines 145–47]

The Law of Moses

One of the central concerns of the New Testament is
to proclaim freedom from an oppressive Jewish
legalism. The devout Jew saw in the law (Torah) God's
demands for his covenant people. The law spelled out
the privileges and responsibilities defining the Jews'
life. Sin was transgression of the law, and righteousness was obedience. The Jews' Scripture was the
unquestioned authority providing their cultural script.
The law's authoritative tone can be heard in the
apodictic Ten Commandments that begin with the
direct address: "Thou shalt . . ."

To safeguard against inadvertent transgression of
divine commandments, the Jews developed additional
precepts. The Pharisaical teachers understood their task
as: "Be deliberate in judgement, raise up disciples, and
make a fence around the Law" (Pirke Aboth 1:45). By
increasing the rules, they sought to bring all of men's
actions under the sovereignty of God. The additional
rules fencing in the ancient law became more numerous
and more difficult to know and to keep. There
developed an inevitable trend toward preoccupation
with the minutia of the law and a corresponding loss of

its inner purpose.[4] Jesus pointed out that the Pharisees have tithed the seasonings, "mint and dill and cummin, and have neglected the weightier matters of the law, justice and mercy and faith; these you ought to have done, without neglecting the others. You blind guides, straining out a gnat and swallowing a camel!" (Matt. 23:23-24).

Many Pharisees, and the common people as well, defined righteousness in terms of conformity to the law and exchanged its true meaning for external forms. They were blind guides substituting show for genuine piety. They were "like whitewashed tombs, which outwardly appear beautiful, but within . . . are full of dead men's bones and all uncleanness" (Matt. 23:27). Religion became a game to manipulate public opinion and even God. Praying in the synagogues and streets (Matt. 6:5), disfiguring of faces while fasting (Matt. 6:16) were displays of piety calculated to gain public acclaim. These religious leaders were pious frauds who obeyed the rules but missed the purpose of the law. "They do all their deeds to be seen by men," Jesus observed, "for they make their phylacteries broad and their fringes long, and they love the place of honor at feasts and the best seats in the synagogues, and salutations in the market places, and being called rabbi by men" (Matt. 23:5-7).

Unthinking conformity to legal authority distorted the real intention of the law.[5] The Pharisees were strict and uncompromising in their demand for obedience from their disciples. Jesus considered their religious requirements to be an oppressive obligation. "They bind heavy burdens, hard to bear, and lay them on men's shoulders" (Matt. 23:4). They were blind to the realization that Jesus' ministry was in actuality a demonstration of the values supporting the law. Because the Pharisees could not understand the God who gave the law, they "shut the kingdom of heaven against men; for you," Jesus said, "neither enter yourselves, nor allow those who would enter to go in" (Matt. 23:13). In their eagerness to make disciples the Pharisees traversed sea and land. Once they had placed the yoke of the law on their poor proselyte, they made him twice the son of hell that they were (Matt. 23:15). "And if a blind man leads a blind man, both will fall into a pit" (Matt. 15:14; cf. John 9:39-41).

Legalism also led the Pharisees to justify neglecting the needs of their own fathers and mothers in order to make charitable gifts to God's service. "So, for the sake of your tradition," Jesus complains, "you have made void the word of God" (Matt. 15:6). They had truly fulfilled the ancient prophecy of Isaiah:

> This people honors me with their lips,
> but their heart is far from me;
> in vain do they worship me,
> teaching as doctrines the precepts of men.

(Matt. 15:8-9; cf. Isa. 29:13)

The Gospel of Matthew obviously reflects the synagogue debate that arose between Jews and Christians during the half-century following the crucifixion. Matthew preserves and underscores the conflict between Jesus and the Jewish leaders that resulted in his crucifixion. It is significant that while Matthew presents Jesus as a new lawgiver like Moses, the evangelist warns against the danger of legalism.

Synagogue debate also influences the Gospel of John, which consistently portrays the orthodox Jewish leaders as insensible to the meaning of the Old Testament Scripture. These Jews do not discern that Jesus' words and works are witnessed to in their own sacred writings. "You search the scriptures," Jesus rebukes, "because you think that in them you have eternal life; and it is they that witness to me; yet you refuse to come to me that you may have life" (John 5:39-40). Jesus understood the import of the law. He lived the meaning of the Torah. "If you believed Moses, you would believe me, for he wrote of me. But if you do not believe his writings, how will you believe my words?" (John 5:46-47).

The blindness of the Jewish leaders is seen further in the sign revealed by Jesus' healing a man *born* blind. They cannot observe the power of God, because the healing violated their sabbath law. Their own perception was so contaminated by legalism that they judged Jesus to be a sinner instead of proclaiming him a man of God. But, their condemnation of Jesus was in effect a judgment of themselves. "Jesus said, 'For judgment I came into this world, that those who do not see may see, and that those who see may become blind.' Some of the Pharisees near him heard this, and they said to him, 'Are we also blind?' Jesus said to them, 'If you were blind, you would have no guilt; but now that you say, "We see," your guilt remains'" (John 9:39-41).

The apostle Paul was reared in a devout Pharisaical home where the law was an authoritative guide to faith and practice. He points out that his parents had circumcised him on the eighth day following his birth, just as the law prescribed (Phil. 3:5). This same scrupulous observance of the law characterized Paul's earliest training. He recalled that "I advanced in Judaism beyond many of my own age among my people, so extremely zealous was I for the traditions of my fathers" (Gal. 1:14). So meticulous was his conformity to the law that he can say of his Jewish life: "As to righteousness under the law blameless" (Phil. 3:6). The book of Acts supports this picture of Paul's youth by his statement to the Jews in Jerusalem "I am a Jew . . . educated according to the strict manner of the law of our fathers, being zealous for God as you all are this day" (Acts 22:3). In his defense before King Agrippa, Paul describes his former zeal for the law, stating that "according to the strictest party of our religion I have lived as a Pharisee" (Acts 26:5).

The zeal that Paul expressed in his strict observance of the letter of the law also compelled him to persecute the Jewish Christians who did not share his fanatical loyalty. Later, as a Christian, Paul remembered his persecutions of the first Christians and realized that his loyalty to the law as an unquestioned authority had caused those atrocities (Gal. 1:13; Phil. 3:6; I Cor. 15:9). He could see that his own Jewish people continued to be zealous for God by their legalism but that they were not enlightened (Rom. 10:2). Their Adult (reason) was contaminated with their Parent (law).

In Romans 7:7-25 Paul reveals in a very personal way his own experience with the law. This is a pivotal passage for understanding Paul's personality and gospel. His confession is based on his own introspective examination of the experience of alienation and salvation relative to the law. The specific formulation of his thoughts in this text has doubtless been shaped by debates in the synagogue.

Paul recalls, "I was once alive apart from the law, but when the commandment came, sin revived and I died; the very commandment which promised life proved to be death to me" (Rom. 7:9-10). There was a time in Paul's early childhood when his Natural Child was free from the Parent law. He was in touch with his feelings, and his behavior was spontaneous and uninhibited. To be "alive" does not mean that he did not experience Not OK feelings or the alienation inherited from Adam (Rom. 5:12-14). He is alive from the deadening effect of legal conformity.

In time Paul's parents taught him the legal script that defined their own lives. Paul understood. I can be OK, if I obey the law. The promise of life, Ok-ness before God, was held forth as his reward, if he adapted to the law's demand. Experiencing Not-OK-ness and coveting OK-ness, Paul zealously conformed to the law and advanced beyond many his own age (Gal. 1:14). His Natural Child rapidly adapted to the law now internalized in his own Parent ego state. Keeping the law became the means of manipulating God to grant salvation. In other words, the Natural Child prompted by Not OK feelings adapted to the Parent in order to achieve OK-ness. The more the Natural Child gives way to the Adapted Child, the greater is the experience of lifelessness. "The very commandment which promised life proved to be death to me" (Rom. 7:10).

"For sin," the selfish effort to manipulate another for a payoff, "finding opportunity in the commandment, deceived me and by it killed me" (Rom. 7:11). From a theological perspective religious legalism produces death because it causes its adherents to trust in their own ability to obtain salvation by conforming to the law.[6] From a psychological point of view legalism is deadening because the Natural Child is oppressed by an authoritative Parent without the use of the Adult. The legalistic fanatic loses sight of his goal and redoubles his effort. "For the written code kills," but as we shall see "the Spirit gives life" (II Cor. 3:6).

The law itself created a dilemma from which Paul could not escape. The law said: "You shall not covet." But, the law's promise of life for those who would obey stimulated in Paul "all kinds of covetousness" (Rom. 7:8). The Not OK Child *wants* OK-ness! Paul's experience of alienation caused him to covet life—salvation. The law revealed and revived sin by increasing the desire for life and tempting Paul to trust in his own ability to attain it. Then the law demanded that Paul deny his selfish motivation for obedience. The result was to lay bare the selfishness and egocentricity intrinsic to human nature.

Is the law, then, the cause of Paul's problem? No! "The law is holy, and the commandment is holy and just and good" (Rom. 7:12). The demands of the law are spiritual, requiring the love of another in order to fulfill them (Rom. 7:14). "Love does no wrong to a neighbor; therefore love is the fulfilling of the law" (Rom. 13:10). The solution to Paul's tension is not to block out the Parent and let his Child be unrestrained. This would be antinomianism and would lead to destructive and unethical conduct. But, Paul realized that he was carnal—"sold under sin"—and that his motivation for keeping the law had not been love of others but love of self and the desire to obtain the payoff of righteousness before God.

Strict conformity to the law as if to an unquestionable

authority had created a strong Parent in Paul and retarded the development of his Adult. His Natural Child had given way to the Adapted Child dominated by the Parent. Paul experienced this conformity as death and the intensification of Not OK feelings. The result of his legalism was that his Adult experienced Parent contamination. Paul expresses his own experience of Adult contamination by confessing, "I do not understand my own actions" (Rom. 7:15). With his Adult he agreed with the law that had been internalized into his Parent. But, he also felt his covetous Child rebelling against the law's proscription of covetousness. Paul's Child wanted the promise of OK-ness before God, and Paul experienced a Parent-Child struggle in which his Adult was so contaminated that he actually lost control of his actions. Paul experienced this loss of Adult control as the power of sin taking hold of his existence. He could will what was right, but the inner struggle between Parent and Child contaminated his Adult and made it impossible for him to behave as he thought best. "For I delight in the law of God, in my inmost self, but I see in my members another law at war with the law of my mind and making me captive to the law of sin which dwells in my members" (Rom. 7:22-23).

Thomas Oden's paraphrase of Romans 7:18b-24 is exceptionally clear and helpful.

> Although I may have a certain intention to do the good, I cannot seem to do it. For the good, toward which my Adult points me and to which I want to consent, I fail to do. Instead I do the very thing which is against my Adult. When my Adult is contaminated in this way, it is as if I

have <u>two wills which conflict: my Parent which tells me what I ought to do, and my Child which tells me what I want to do</u>. My Adult reality-orientation is caught helplessly in the middle, so much so that you might say that it is not exactly "I" who am doing what I prefer not to do, but rather it is my adapted Child colluding with the archaic Parent lodging in my consciousness. Just at the point at which I know what is right, the only thing within my reach seems to be the Parent tape with which I have colluded. It is as if I am scripted to do the wrong thing, to be a loser.

In my inmost self I continue to be in touch with reality, but in my bodily behavior it seems as if something else is at work, a different momentum which fights against the law of my Adult, the data of which my reason approves. This, in effect makes me a prisoner, locking me into my own archaic collusions. Under these conditions, I despair over my whole existence. I cry out for deliverance from this compulsive bondage of my will which seems to be scripting me to futility and death. I hear a gallows laugh echoing out of my own scripted consciousness. What possible new avenue might be open to me?[7]

In this struggle, experienced as being enslaved by demonic powers, Paul cries out: "Wretched man that I am! Who will deliver me from this body of death?" (Rom. 7:24). From his agony Paul declares relief: "Thanks be to God through Jesus Christ our Lord!" (Rom. 7:25). How then does Jesus Christ provide the escape from the demonic power of sin and legalism?

VI
Grace and OK-ness

There is therefore now no condemnation for those who are in Christ Jesus.

—*Romans 8:1*

In the Cross, Paul discovered the grace of God releasing him from the power of sin. "For God has done what the law, weakened by the flesh, could not do: sending his own Son in the likeness of sinful flesh and for sin, he condemned sin in the flesh, in order that the just requirement of the law might be fulfilled in us, who walk not according to the flesh but according to the Spirit" (Rom. 8:3-4). Through the death of Jesus, Paul caught sight of the creative source of human life—love and acceptance. He came to realize that there was nothing in reality to justify his feelings of alienation.

Paul's experience of God's grace led him to change his legalistic script from: "I can be OK if I keep the commandments" to "I am OK because God loves me." The conviction that God accepts sinful man opened the way to life. "There is therefore now no condemnation for those who are in Christ Jesus" (Rom. 8:1). This is the liberating Christian proclamation. Our OK-ness does not depend on our achievements but rather on God's unmerited favor. In the Cross of Jesus, God declared: "You are OK!" Paul's conversion transformed him from a person seeking for acceptance to a person seeking within acceptance.

This transformation may be illustrated by a story that I occasionally tell my students. It is a true story—not in the sense that it happened once—but in the more profound sense that it happens often.

Once upon a time, a five-year-old girl was dressed in her nightgown, all ready to go to bed. Her father took her into his arms and sat her on his lap. He asked her if she wanted him to buy her a present when he went to town the next day. Her brightly scrubbed face grew even more radiant with anticipation. "Yes!" she said, "I want the doll that I saw in the toy store window." The father agreed and off to bed she went.

The next morning the father hurried to finish his breakfast in order to catch the train to town. The little girl came sleepily to the table, climbed onto her chair, picked at her oatmeal, and carelessly turned over a full glass of milk on her father's freshly pressed suit pants. He jumped up and quickly wiped the milk away. In haste and disgust he strode out the front door. As he reached the bottom of the steps that led to the sidewalk, he heard a scream behind him. Turning, he saw his little girl running after him with tears streaming down her cheeks. He stooped and lifted her again into his arms as he heard her cry: "Are you still going to give me the dolly?"

With your mind's eye place the face of the little girl the evening before beside her expression at the foot of the steps. Why the difference? The contrast is between seeking within acceptance and seeking for acceptance.

Both Transactional Analysis and the New Testament point toward the experience of grace or OK-ness as the source of authentic life. T.A. recognizes that the initial emotional position assumed by every infant is I'm Not

OK—You're OK. This position may change during the first years to one of two alternative emotional positions: I'm Not OK—You're Not OK or I'm OK—You're Not OK. There is, however, a fourth position—that taken by the mentally healthy person—which is, I'm OK—You're OK. The first three emotional positions are preverbal and unconscious; the fourth is an Adult *decision* or act of faith based on evidence. It is an intelligent decision based on a vast amount of information that was unavailable when the infant assumed the attitude of I'm Not OK—You're OK. The fourth position can also deal with the possibilities of what might be. It can raise the philosophical and religious questions concerning the worth of individuals and the ultimate purpose of men's lives. *"The first three positions are based on feelings. The fourth is based on thought, faith, and the wager of action."* [1]

The I'm OK—You're OK position is not one that we drift into; rather it is a rational Adult decision to live with the conviction that life and people are valuable as ends in themselves. This stance makes it possible to begin the Adult process of collecting accurate data, estimating probabilities, and making intelligent decisions. We can begin a new set of transactions that will start us toward a successful life-style. The Not-OK Child feelings are not erased, and certain stress situations may trigger the negative feelings again. But when these archaic feelings do replay, we can recognize them using our Adult reasoning as archaic Child feelings that no longer correspond to reality and thus dispose of them.

The I'm OK—You're OK position does not resolve all human conflict immediately. Others will continue to play games and occasionally they may "hook" our

Child or Parent. But, the Adult position provides the stance for dealing with reality rationally, minimizing conflicts, and developing constructive interpersonal relationships. The goal of these relations is to stop playing games and achieve an intimacy based on the worth of self and others; that is, loving your neighbor *and* yourself.

The central salvific message of the T.A. therapist is: I'm OK—You're OK. There is in T.A. an implicit philosophical assumption about the nature of reality. The I'm OK—You're OK position corresponds to reality and is the position of healthy individuals, winners, and "decent folk." This position is intrinsically constructive because it places the Adult in charge of one's life and makes it possible to deal thoughtfully with present reality, as well as with archaic Parent data and Child feelings. This position is considered *to be in tune with the reality of things.* Thomas Oden has correctly observed of T.A., "Thus it becomes an ontological statement, a statement about being, about the way things *are*. When we are most in touch with the real situation in which we exist, we affirm ourselves and others." [2]

T.A. makes tacit ontological assumptions, that is, assumes that the I'm OK—You're OK position puts one in touch with reality. "Any time we concern ourselves with personality growth, we make assumptions about the good and the real (ethics and ontology). We define health in terms of what is most reality-oriented, and thus most in touch with actual being itself." [3] My OK-ness does not merely depend on another's saying so, not even the T.A. therapist's, although another person may assist me in making this Adult decision.

Furthermore, my Adult decision is not canceled by the negative appraisals of others. *OK-ness is ultimately grounded in the nature of being itself.* T.A. then points toward a doctrine of God as grace and love. However, since T.A. is concerned to analyze the structure of the self and the nature of interpersonal transactions, it cannot explicate its own theological implications. The New Testament, on the other hand, begins with the conviction that God is sovereign love and proceeds to spell out the implications of this for salvation, ethics, and community.

The Gospels portray Jesus as the man who uniquely discloses God as a forgiving and loving Father. Jesus' message and ministry was an historical example of I'm OK—You're OK. He claimed that OK-ness was grounded in a merciful God who accepts the unworthy. Jesus lived in a society where most people made a sharp distinction between those who were righteous and those not favored by God—the sick, the possessed, the poor, and the sinful. In this society the respectable were so insecure in their self-righteousness they could not risk involvement with the unclean. But, Jesus extended acceptance to those rejected by society and claimed that the fellowship that he offered would be valid before God. It was the understanding that God is merciful that was the heart of Jesus' ministry. This knowledge provided the authority that so amazed Jesus' audiences when he healed the sick, cast out demons, and reinterpreted the law.

Jesus proclaimed that the kingdom of heaven was at hand, not simply because time had run out as the apocalyptists believed, but because time could be filled with meaning derived from the nearness of a compas-

71

sionate God. Would not the God who cares when a sparrow falls be concerned also with fallen man made in God's own image (Matt. 10:29-31; Luke 12:6-7)? It was to the people weighed down by the experience of alienation that Jesus particularly addressed his message. The Gospel of Luke introduces the ministry of Jesus with a passage from Isaiah (61:1-2) read by Jesus in the synagogue at Nazareth.

> The Spirit of the Lord is upon me, because he has anointed me to preach good news to the poor. He has sent me to proclaim release to the captives and recovering of sight to the blind, to set at liberty those who are oppressed, to proclaim the acceptable year of the Lord. (Luke 4:18-19)

Jesus returned the book to the attendant and announced: "Today this scripture has been fulfilled in your hearing."

The Gospel of Mark emphasizes the authority that characterized Jesus' ministry. The power that Jesus displayed amazed the people and caused consternation in those leaders whose position Jesus challenged. Mark (2:1-12) points out that the authority of Jesus to forgive sins (i.e., to proclaim You're OK before God) and to heal are one and the same. The story is told of Jesus' return to his home in Capernaum. While Jesus taught, a large crowd gathered, filling the house and blocking the door. A paralytic was carried by four men who, being unable to enter the door, lowered the paralyzed man through the roof. Observing their faith, Jesus said to the man: "My son, your sins are forgiven." The scribes who witnessed this offer of forgiveness thought that

Jesus blasphemed, since only God could forgive sins. Jesus responded to their critical judgment: "Why do you question thus in your hearts? Which is easier, to say to the paralytic, 'Your sins are forgiven,' or to say, 'Rise, take up your pallet and walk'?" To demonstrate his authority over both sin and sickness Jesus said to the paralytic: "I say to you rise, take up your pallet and go home." The man did as he was told, to the amazement of the onlookers.

The story of the paralytic reveals the close association between Jesus' pronouncement of OK-ness and his power to heal. Those in the first century who were burdened with the script that human misfortune equalled divine disapproval received from Jesus a display of compassion. He encouraged the oppressed with the words: "Come to me, all who labor and are heavy laden, and I will give you rest" (Matt. 11:28). He accepted the unfortunate and proclaimed that God's love extended especially to them. Jesus' works and words disclosed the benevolent and creative source of all life, and he invited his hearers to live joyfully in this new awareness.

Jesus also manifested his authority over the demons who took possession of people's lives. In the first-century prescientific culture, mental illness was attributed to demon possession. When Jesus' contemporaries apprehended that a power was taking control of their minds and causing irrational language and behavior, they believed that it could only be the work of a demon. Vernon McCasland in his book *By The Finger of God* has explored the types of mental illness described in the New Testament as demon possession.[4] (McCasland's research influenced the best-selling novel by William P.

73

Jesus deviated from the script ∴ is the script true?

Blatty *The Exorcist*.)[5] Jesus confronted the demoniacs with an authority derived from understanding the nature of reality as love. He commanded the demons to go out and leave men to live freely in the knowledge that God is Father.

T.A. has provided some interesting insights and useful vocabulary for describing demon possession in our modern world. Through our present understanding of the structure of the self we can more clearly grasp the phenomenon described in the New Testament and the nature of Jesus' healing power. Jesus by his affirmation of OK-ness in God's name helped people whose Adult was contaminated by Not-OK Child feelings or archaic Parent data to gain control of their lives by reactivating their Adult.

Recently in *Psychology Today* an article by Fanita English indirectly cast light on the healing power that was effected by Jesus' authoritative pronouncement of OK-ness. Clinical practice has repeatedly discovered that the intelligent and well-educated modern can be under a demonic spell as strong as that of first-century man. Not OK feelings within the Child can on occasion contaminate the Adult and cause loss of control. "A person experiences a 'curse' as a flooding of 'I'm Not OK, You're Not OK' feelings with despair, desolation, hopelessness and total lack of trust. Irrational magical thinking takes over."[6]

How can one be released from these troll messages or the curse of demon possession?

In such cases, magic must be countered with magic. Nothing short of exorcism will do, to be followed by new fairy-godmother permissions. To exorcise the curse, the therapist puts on a "Merlin"; i.e., she takes on a magical all-powerful Parental role to deal with the patients' Spooky [fearful] Child. She indicates that she (the therapist) is more powerful than the old witch, who is way back in the six-year-old realm. The therapist reminds the Child that she has a new guardian of her own—her own grown-up self that enables her to use physical mobility and elementary know-how to survive.[7]

It was the authoritative pronouncement of man's OK-ness before God that was the source of Jesus' therapeutic power. This same authority was considered to be blasphemy by the Jewish leaders, whose Adult was contaminated by their archaic traditions. Jesus' declarations of forgiveness were coupled with the permission to live: "Rise, take up your pallet and go home" (Mark 2:11). "Neither do I condemn you; go and do not sin again" (John 8:11).

> The therapist bestows permissions: Permission to feel what you feel! Permission to *know* how you feel! Permission to seek out and recognize real strokes! Permission to enjoy! Permission to *live*! And permission to not *hurt yourself!*[8]

The Gospel writers do not represent Jesus healing every disease; his power to heal was not automatic. Mark relates how Jesus when he came to his own home "could do no mighty work there, except that he laid his hands upon a few sick people and healed them" (Mark 6:5). In this instance Jesus, not the crowd, was the one who marveled—marveled at their unbelief. The ability to heal the sick and cast out demons was not Jesus' alone. He gave this authority to his disciples (Mark

3:15; 6:7-13) and at least one man who was not among their number could cast out demons by the authority of Jesus' name (Mark 9:38-41). In a world script laden with guilt and Not-OK-ness, an authoritative pronouncement of OK-ness in God's name could heal. The same is true today!

The kingdom of God that Jesus proclaimed had to be met with faith that God's grace was at work in the world. Faith as small as a mustard seed could produce extraordinary results (Matt. 17:20; Luke 17:6). The Gospel writers are witnesses to the power that Jesus manifested; they were convinced that his life disclosed to men the power of life grounded in God. His was not the life of just a good man, another miracle worker, an apocalyptist preacher, or an itinerant rabbi. Jesus revealed God as a merciful Father and challenged men to share the experience of OK-ness. "Be merciful, even as your Father is merciful" (Luke 6:36). He was the Son of God because his life culminating in the Cross revealed the source of true human life as love. The Gospel writers selected their materials from the oral tradition containing various stories about Jesus. They appropriated these stories and embellished their miraculous nature with profound theological awareness; Jesus' life and ministry had become transparent to the very Ground of Being. The Gospels are a unique meld of historical narrative and theological interpretation that cannot be separated without destroying the significance of Jesus Christ. T.A. does not provide categories that can deal adequately with the faith of the early Christians in Jesus as the revelation of God. But, T.A.'s emphasis on the I'm OK—You're OK position as the stance of the healthy reality-oriented individual is consistent with the reality revealed by Jesus' ministry.

The Gospel of John focuses on Jesus as the incarnation of the *Logos*, the creative Word of God. John uses signs to open his readers' eyes to the significance of the wonders performed by Jesus. Each sign points beyond itself to the reality of God as love. "For God so loved the world that he gave his only Son, that whoever believes in him should not perish but have eternal life" (John 3:16). The love of God for man provides the OK-ness that removes the Not-OK Child fears and makes a healthy life possible. "God is love, and he who abides in love abides in God, and God abides in him. . . . There is no fear in love, but perfect love casts out fear" (I John 4:16, 18). Faith in God's love for man makes possible man's love for his brother. "We love, because he first loved us. . . . And this commandment we have from him, that he who loves God should love his brother also" (I John 4:19, 21). This is the Adult position: I'm OK—You're OK. "No man has ever seen God; if we love one another, God abides in us and his love is perfected in us" (I John 4:12). Jesus said that when his disciple lives in the power of God's love he will not only be able to do what Jesus does, but "greater works than these will he do" (John 14:12).

Paul shares Jesus' focus on God's grace as the hope for alienated mankind. He discovered through the Cross that the grace of God is the power to overcome sin. OK-ness or justification is a gift from God and not a human achievement based on conformity to the law (Rom. 4:4). "For there is no distinction; since all have sinned and fall short of the glory of God, they are justified by his grace as a gift, through the redemption which is in Christ Jesus, whom God put forward as an expiation by his blood, to be received by faith" (Rom. 3:22-25). The faith decision to accept the righteousness that comes from God removed the Not-OK Child fears that plagued Paul's life. Grace removed his anxiety. "Therefore, since we are justified by faith, we have peace with God through our Lord Jesus Christ" (Rom. 5:1).

Faith in the sovereign love of God granted to Paul a deep sense of security and victory over the powers that threatened him. "For I am sure that neither death, nor life, nor angels, nor principalities, nor things present, nor things to come, nor powers, nor height, nor depth, nor anything else in all creation, will be able to separate us from the love of God in Christ Jesus our Lord" (Rom. 8:38-39). The Child feelings of Not-OK-ness were turned off through the conviction that God bestows OK-ness as a gift; the Natural Child is freed from an authoritative legalism. "Through [Jesus] we have obtained access to this grace in which we stand, and we rejoice in our hope of sharing the glory of God" (Rom. 5:2; cf. 5:11).

Various images are employed by Paul to express the experience of OK-ness derived from faith in God's grace. It is like a slave who has been adopted as a son into the family of God (Rom. 8:14-17). The Cross is viewed as a cultic sacrifice that appeases an angry God and effects a reconciliation (Rom. 3:24-26). The experience of OK-ness is like that felt by a criminal who hears the judge pronounce his acquital (Rom. 5:18). With these images Paul stresses the good news that there is nothing in reality to justify the Not OK feelings that once frustrated his life. Since Paul was justified by faith in God's grace, he was free from the necessity to keep the law as a means of obtaining justification. "For we hold that a man is justified by faith apart from works of the law" (Rom. 3:28).

What becomes of the law? "Do we then overthrow the law by this faith?" (Rom. 3:31). How can we be free from the obligation to conform to Parent-law authority without becoming irresponsible and unethical?

VII
Love and the Adult

Think not that I have come to abolish the law and the prophets; I have come not to abolish them but to fulfill them.

—Matthew 5:17

The ethic of the New Testament is in large measure an Adult updating of the law in the light of God's love. The authority that Jesus manifested by healings and exorcisms was also directed toward reinterpreting the law. He was critical of the legalism of the orthodox Jewish leaders because it obscured the reality toward which the law pointed. However, Jesus' rejection of legalism should not be confused with rejecting the law itself—antinomianism.

The Jewish teachers in their attempt to bring all of men's conduct under the sovereignty of God increased the number of commandments. Jesus shared with the pious Jew the concern to bring all of life under God's rule. But, Jesus sought to accomplish this goal by bringing men's hearts under God's sovereignty. Human life is to be a sharing of divine compassion. The rabbis' interpretations of the law were based on extensive oral traditions. What a specific text meant was worked out in the context of a chain of earlier interpretations and precedents. Much rabbinic teaching was so complicated and erudite that only a professional lawyer could follow the legal arguments. Jesus, on the other hand, gave authoritative interpretations of the law's meaning not by citing other authorities but by appealing to the nature of God as Father, the ultimate giver of the law. That is, Jesus directed the attention of his hearers away from meticulous performance and toward justice, mercy, and faith (Matt. 23:23).

The Gospel of Matthew demonstrates the authoritative manner in which Jesus treats the law. Matthew is divided into five major sections that parallel the Mosaic Torah, the Pentateuch. Just as Moses received the law on the holy mountain Sinai, so the evangelist places Jesus on the mountain to give an authoritative reinterpretation of the law. The Sermon on the Mount is essentially an updating of archaic Jewish traditions in the Adult realization that God is compassionate. Jesus' teaching is not an abrogation of the law, but rather a fulfilling of the law's inner intent. His radical ethic shines forth in the demand: "You, therefore, must be perfect, as your heavenly Father is perfect" (Matt. 5:48). Jesus outlegalized the legalist by bringing not only the deed but also the motive under the sovereignty of God. "For I tell you, unless your righteousness exceeds that of the scribes and Pharisees, you will never enter the kingdom of heaven" (Matt. 5:20).

Matthew casts the teachings of Jesus in the linguistic form "You have heard that it was said to the men of old . . ." The archaic Parent data from the Ten Commandments and Jewish casuistry is then updated as Jesus says: "But I say to you . . ." The law forbade murder, but Jesus censures hatred (Matt. 5:21-22). The law proscribed adultery, but Jesus condemns lust (Matt. 5:27-28). The law stipulated not to swear falsely, but Jesus commends speaking with simplicity and integrity (Matt. 5:33-37). The law expressed an understanding of

81

deed vs. motive
Ex, murder vs. hate

justice based on revenge, *lex talionis*; it required "an eye for an eye and a tooth for a tooth." Jesus teaches that justice is best served by sharing the mercy of God. "Do not resist one who is evil. But if any one strikes you on the right cheek, turn to him the other also" (Matt. 5:39). If you are sued in a court of law and lose your coat, give the plaintiff your cloak too. If you are compelled to go one mile, go a second mile voluntarily. "Love your enemies and pray for those who persecute you." (Matt. 5:44).

Jesus' attitude toward keeping the law is revealed in an encounter with a rich man who ran up to Jesus and inquired: "Good Teacher, what must I do to inherit eternal life?" (Mark 10:17-22; Matt. 19:16-22; Luke 18:18-23). Jesus replied that the man knew the Ten Commandments and should observe them. But, the rich man insisted that he had kept these from his youth, and yet he sensed that something more ought to be done. Jesus observed the man's dedication and loved him. "You lack one thing," Jesus responded; "Go, sell what you have, and give to the poor, and you will have treasure in heaven; and come, follow me." The man went away sorrowful because he could not surrender his wealth.

Jesus' directive exposed the basic selfishness that motivated the rich man's obedience to the law. The man felt Not OK even after conforming to the law. He asked Jesus how he could become OK before God. Jesus required of the man a self-sacrificial act that exposed his basic selfishness. Not until he experienced the OK-ness that is grounded in God's mercy could he be free from his legalism and greed. Legalism seeks through collecting "good works" to become OK; greed seeks through

82

collecting "good things" to become OK. This rich Jew was accomplished in both, and yet he was aware that true life had escaped him. Jesus invited this man to the freedom of discipleship, where his sense of self-worth would be derived from being a son of a merciful Father. The rich man might have learned that "it is more blessed to give than to receive" (Acts 20:35) because giving shares in God's creative love.

Jesus' understanding of the law is also revealed in the story of a lawyer (Luke 10:25-37) who stood up and tested Jesus with the question: "Teacher, what shall I do to inherit eternal life?" Jesus recognized him to be a learned man and so responded: "What is written in the law? How do you read?" The lawyer's answer was no less astute than it was succinct. He combined a passage from Deuteronomy 6:5 with Leviticus 19:18 and said that the law is fulfilled by loving God with your whole being and loving "your neighbor as yourself." Jesus agreed: "Do this, and you will live."

But, the lawyer, encouraged by his initial success, pressed his case. Using a typically legalistic approach, he sought to establish the limits of his liability. "And who is my neighbor?" the lawyer inquired. That is, where does the sphere of my responsibility end? Jesus told the parable of the Good Samaritan who aided an unfortunate Jew, beaten and robbed, after both priest and Levite had passed him by. Then Jesus interrogated the lawyer as to which of the three men proved to be a neighbor to the assaulted man. The lawyer drew the unavoidable conclusion: "The one who showed mercy on him." Jesus had altered the lawyer's perspective from attempting to draw a limit on love's response to seeking to inspire love in each interpersonal relationship. In this context the law is fulfilled when a person—any person, even a Samaritan—assumes an Adult I'm OK—You're OK position and acts accordingly. "Go," Jesus said, "and do likewise."

The Gospel of John contrasts the divine requirement set forth by Jesus' ministry with the blind legalism of orthodox Judaism. The prologue introduces this leading motif with the words: "For the law was given through Moses; grace and truth came through Jesus Christ" (John 1:17). The Jews in their legalism were actually not observing the true meaning of the law (John 7:19-24). Jesus claimed to disclose the God who had given the law. He dared to call God his Father! In the name of law and order the Jews put Jesus to death and justified their action by stating: "We have a law, and by that law he ought to die, because he has made himself the Son of God" (John 19:7, cf. 10:31-39; 12:34). But even the Jews' blind hatred of Jesus is understood by him as a fulfillment of their law (John 15:25).

In the place of the legalism that contaminated the Jews' Adult appraisal of Jesus, the Gospel of John presents Jesus' declaration of a new kind of commandment. "This is my commandment," Jesus said, "that you love one another as I have loved you" (John 15:12). This commandment stands in sharp contrast to legalism and literalism. To keep Jesus' commandment is truly to be free from literalism, because "if you keep my commandments, you will abide in my love, just as I have kept my Father's commandments and abide in his love" (John 15:10). The new commandment that Jesus gave his followers was to acknowledge their OK-ness before God and share this OK-ness in the world. This may be seen as the transformation from darkness

Legalism can contaminate our "adult"

(Not-OK-ness) to light (OK-ness). It is freedom from the law as Parent but not from morality.

The so-called spurious passage contained in John 8:2-11 illustrates the Johannine understanding of Jesus as one who supersedes the law. The setting appropriately is at the Jerusalem temple early in the morning. As Jesus is teaching, the scribes and Pharisees bring a woman who had been caught in adultery and thrust her before him. They say: "Teacher, this woman has been caught in the act of adultery. Now in the law Moses commanded us to stone such. What do you say about her?" Jesus is placed in a dilemma. Shall he require that the law's punishment be ruthlessly exacted, or shall he teach that the law be ignored? Jesus stoops and writes with his finger on the ground, but his questioners persist. Standing again, Jesus looks directly at those who have brought the adultress and says: "Let him who is without sin among you be the first to throw a stone at her." While he kneels again writing, all leave one by one until only the woman remains. Jesus looks up and inquires about her accusers but she replies that no one remains to condemn her. Then Jesus reveals the Adult way in which he reinterpreted the law. "Neither do I condemn you; go, and do not sin again."

The updating of the Jewish law in the Adult realization that God is love *(agape)* is a central theme of the First Epistle of John. "We love, because [God] first loved us" (I John 4:19). The love of God has been revealed in the Cross of Jesus. "In this is love, not that we loved God but that he loved us and sent his Son to be the expiation for our sins" (I John 4:10). The Adult activated by the security of knowing that God is love makes possible a reevaluation of the old law. The

85

updating of the Mosaic law is expressed by contrasting the old commandments with the new commandment.[1] "Beloved, I am writing you no new commandment, but an old commandment which you had from the beginning; the old commandment is the word which you have heard. Yet I am writing you a new commandment, which is true in him and in you, because the darkness is passing away and the true light is already shining" (I John 2:7-8). The Parent law was updated in the Adult understanding that reality is love. In this way Christianity preserved its continuity with the Jewish heritage while at the same time freeing itself for a new ethic and life-style in which the love revealed in the Cross lived on in the community of faith. "By this we know love, that he laid down his life for us; and we ought to lay down our lives for the brethren" (I John 3:16).

The discovery of God as love is uniquely granted in the Cross. On one side the Cross reveals the nature of God's self-giving love; on the other side the Cross is both a challenge to accept this love as the fulfillment of life and to share love. To know God as love is to be OK; but the knowledge of love requires that we say by word and deed: "You're OK" (I John 3:23-24). "And this commandment we have from him, that he who loves God should love his brother also" (I John 4:21; cf. 5:2-3). The love of another causes us to abide in God and so attain the goal of OK-ness (I John 4:12).

The apostle Paul also came to realize that love fulfills the law. We have seen how Paul attempted to gain OK-ness by conformity to the law as a Parent authority. The more Paul adapted to the requirements of the written code, the greater was his experience of Not-OK-ness. Paul obtained a release from alienation by accepting the Cross as the revelation of God's grace to be received in faith. He felt secure in the conviction that God is sovereign love (Rom. 8:31-39). "There is therefore now no condemnation for those who are in Christ Jesus" (Rom. 8:1). The experience of grace made it possible for Paul to update the content of his Parent. He understood that the purpose of the law was fulfilled by love.[2] "Owe no one anything, except to love one another; for he who loves his neighbor has fulfilled the law" (Rom. 13:8).

Transactional Analysis provides helpful language for restating Paul's relationship to the law. Parent contamination results from a breakdown in the ego boundary separating the Parent from the Adult. Archaic ideas replay in the present without being intelligently examined. These outdated ideas are expressed in the form of *prejudices.* Extreme Parent contamination may produce *hallucinations.*[3] The Adult perceives the Parent

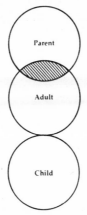

Fig. 5. Parent Contamination of the Adult

voices as originating outside the personality. Usually these voices are threatening or they demand violent actions.

Paul's zealous persecution of the church before embracing Christianity demonstrates the unreasoning attitude that he had initially toward Christians. Paul "with a good conscience" could approve and participate in acts of violence against Christians in order to support the traditions of his fathers. He closed his mind to the prospect that God was at work in the Cross reconciling the world unto himself. Paul would uphold the law even if he must hunt down and destroy his own Jewish brethren who had defected to Christianity. He had heard the gospel concerning Jesus Christ and it had filled him with rage.

The treatment for a Parent-contaminated Adult is to restore the damaged ego boundary. This restoration is not achieved through the use of logical arguments against the prejudice. Rational arguments are ineffective, since it is the Adult that has been impaired by archaic Parent data. The more one argues with a person suffering from Parent contamination, the more defensive and irrational the person will likely become. This is especially true when he believes that his salvation depends on adherence to orthodoxy.

The restoration of the damaged ego boundary can best be accomplished by helping the person to realize that it is no longer dangerous to disagree with the content of his Parent.[4] When a person feels secure to investigate and to evaluate the content of his Parent without fear of punishment or harm, then it is possible to update the archaic data in the light of present reality. Without the awareness that these threatening Parent tapes do not correspond to reality, a person will remain locked in his prejudices.

Paul's discovery of God's grace in the Cross gave him the security that made possible a reappraisal of the Parent law. "For we hold that a man is justified by faith apart from works of law" (Rom. 3:28). "Therefore, since we are justified by faith we have peace with God through our Lord Jesus Christ" (Rom. 5:1). The experience of grace recommissioned Paul's Adult so he could update the law in the light of God's sovereign love. Paul's Adult appraisal of the law was that its basic intention was good, holy, and just (Rom. 7:12). The teachings of the law that were consistent with the understanding of God as love abide. "Love does no wrong to a neighbor; therefore love is the fulfilling of the law" (Rom. 13:10). "For the whole law is fulfilled in one word, 'You shall love your neighbor as yourself'" (Gal. 5:14; James 2:8). Cultic practices, dietary restrictions, circumcision, and Jewish casuistry were no longer obligatory for the mature Christian who lived in the Adult realization that love fills man's life (Rom. 14:5-21; I Cor. 10:19-33). Paul's security as a Christian made it possible for him to update the law and so maintain continuity with his past life in Judaism while at the same time freeing him from the scrupulous legalistic observances. "The commandments, 'You shall not commit adultery, You shall not kill, You shall not steal, You shall not covet,' and any other commandment, are summed up in this sentence, 'You shall love your neighbor as yourself'" (Rom. 13:9). Paul could enlarge on the understanding of love and make an intelligent application of its meaning in order to redeem interpersonal transactions (I Cor. 13:1-3). "Let love be genuine" (Rom. 12:9; cf. Col. 3:14). "The faith that you have, keep between yourself and God; *happy is he who has no reason to judge himself for what he approves*" (Rom. 14:22; italics added).

Love makes possible an updating of the Parent law, but how does the experience of grace affect the Child ego state?

VIII
The Power of the Spirit

Truly, I say to you, unless you turn and become like children, you will never enter the kingdom of heaven.

—*Matthew 18:3*

The acceptance of God's gift of OK-ness frees the Natural Child from the Parent domination of the law. Paul asks the Galatian Christians who were in danger of returning to legalism: "Did you receive the Spirit by works of the law, or by hearing with faith?" (Gal. 3:2). His answer is the latter; the Spirit came by trusting in the new script that man is OK before God. What is the relationship then between experiencing faith in God's pronouncement: "You're OK," and experiencing the power of the Spirit?

We have seen how the Natural Child adapts to the Parent as a taught concept of life. The little person feels helpless and Not OK; he conforms to the dictates of his parents in order to survive and become OK. The initial emotional position I'm Not OK—You're OK leads naturally to the life script: "You can become OK if . . ." As the Natural Child conforms to the Parent ego state the Adapted Child develops. However, Not-OK-ness is not overcome by conformity to the Parent; rather, the stronger the Adapted Child becomes, the more one experiences alienation from personal wholeness. The content of the Parent may be accurate and helpful, but as an authority accepted uncritically (the Adult is not a part of the transaction), the Parent is oppressive. What

91

happens when the Parent is blocked out and the Child feelings are released for uninhibited expression?

The Child ego state contains the feelings recorded during the first years of life; the release of the Adapted Child from Parent domination causes a flood of mixed emotions. The Natural Child is affectionate, spontaneous, and creative; but the Natural Child is also uninhibited, selfish, shameless, cruel, and fearful. The blocking out of the Parent opens a Pandora's box of archaic feelings that can cause destructive behavior. Child contamination of the Adult when the Parent is blocked out may result in psychopathic behavior. The person experiences no restraint or guilt. Anything goes! In extreme cases he may suffer from delusion. He may have the delusion of grandeur and feel, "I can do no wrong!" Or he may suffer from the delusion of persecution and feel, "They are trying to hurt me!"

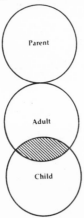

Fig. 6. Child Contamination of the Adult

The Child take-over of the personality is treated by restoring the ego boundary between the Adult and

Child. This restoration cannot be accomplished by mere factual statements, for the Adult has been impaired by Child contamination. To help heal the lesion in the ego boundary it is necessary to reassure the person by pointing out that the archaic Child feelings that are replaying in the present are inappropriate to the present situation. As the Adult is restored to control it will be able to compute reality and decontaminate the affected area. Once the Adult is recommissioned it can determine which feelings are appropriate to the present and which are inappropriate. The Adult can then turn off the archaic and irrelevant Child feelings and turn on the appropriate feelings.[1]

The New Testament's message of freedom is that man is OK before God without having to conform to law. The blocking-out of the Parent law created a release of psychic or spiritual power in the believers, whose Natural Child was liberated by the faith-decision to accept God's grace proclaimed in the gospel. The early Christians were a Spirit-filled community; the new surge of energy they felt in their lives was viewed as a guarantee of God's presence (II Cor. 1:22; 5:5). "What happens, then, in a religious experience?" Thomas Harris asks. "It is my opinion that religious experience may be a unique combination of Child (a feeling of intimacy) and Adult (a reflection on ultimacy) with the total exclusion of the Parent."[2]

Faith in God's grace turned on feelings of affection and intimacy in the first Christians. This outbreak of enthusiasm accompanied the experience of well-being resulting from the conviction that God is sovereign love. Paul contrasted the experience of reconciliation with the old feelings of alienation. The fear and estrangement of the slave were replaced by the OK-ness and acceptance of a son. "For all who are led by the Spirit of God are sons of God" (Rom. 8:14). The Natural Child feelings of security and affection are set free by faith in God's grace.

Paul recalls the intimate Aramaic word "Abba," by which he as a child had addressed his own father. This highly charged emotional word appropriately expresses the feelings that accompany the presence of the Spirit. "When we cry, 'Abba! Father!' it is the Spirit himself bearing witness with our spirit that we are children of God, and if children, then heirs, heirs of God and fellow heirs with Christ" (Rom. 8:15-17). Paul emphasizes that the gift of the Spirit accompanies the realization of sonship, OK-ness. When the dominating Parent is blocked out by the Adult decision I'm OK, the Natural Child is freed. This release is experienced as freedom and power. "And because you are sons, God has sent the Spirit of his Son into our hearts, crying, Abba! Father!' So through God you are no longer a slave but a son, and if a son then an heir" (Gal. 4:6-7).

The experience of OK-ness grants an openness toward life and hope for the future. The Christian views the present as pregnant with possibility (Rom. 8:22).[3] The conviction that I'm OK liberates a depth of feelings and creative energy that is more primitive and complex than reason (the Adult). "Likewise the Spirit helps us in our weakness; for we do not know how to pray as we ought, but the Spirit himself intercedes for us with sighs too deep for words" (Rom. 8:26). Even the Child feelings are redeemed through the recognition that God affirms man's OK-ness. Paul sums up his joyful message of salvation in the words:

> Therefore, since we are justified by faith, we have peace with God through our Lord Jesus Christ. Through him we have obtained access to this grace in which we stand, and we rejoice in our hope of sharing the glory of God. . . . Hope does not disappoint us, because God's love has been poured into our hearts through the Holy Spirit which has been given to us. (Rom. 5:1-2, 5)

Muriel James and Louis M. Savary have correctly observed in their recent book *The Power at the Bottom of the Well* that the psychic energy released by a healthy I'm OK—You're OK position is akin to the gift of the Spirit described in the New Testament. They term this spiritual energy the "Power Within." "Others may prefer to call the source of this inner power God, Spirit, Nature, Ground of Being, or some other name. Paul the apostle was referring to the Power Within when he asked, Do you know that God's Spirit dwells in you?' "[4]

Paul realizes that faith in God's grace frees man from bondage to the law and results in the gift of the Spirit. However, Paul is concerned that Christian liberty be more than just the release of Dionysiac urges. The Spirit of Christ produces an updating of Child feelings in the awareness that reality is Love. Those feelings that are appropriate to the Spirit of Love are given free reign; those feelings that are based on fear and Not-OK-ness are turned off. The concern to define spiritual gifts in terms of God's love preoccupies Paul's attention in much of I Corinthians. Life in the Spirit means the freedom to love and the dissolution of legal definitions of ethical responsibility. "To give and to respect freedom is, in fact, the work of the Holy Spirit, and the Holy Spirit is rarely comfortable and never without surprises; indeed, it often brings disrepute with it," writes Ernst Käsemann, who has given special attention to early Christian enthusiasm. "There is no Christian freedom without a dose of enthusiasm; and today, after long abstention, that dose ought to be generous rather than meagre, even if the result should be slight intoxication."[5]

There were some members of the church at Corinth who believed that Christian liberty meant not only freedom from the law but freedom for selfish indulgence—that is, antinomianism. They took the position: "All things are lawful for me" (I Cor. 6:12, 10:23). Paul points out that they are free from legalism, but not from the responsibility to love. He actually describes their behavior as immature and childlike, "as babes in Christ" (I Cor. 3:1). Their Not-OK Child state was expressed by playing the game of "Mine Is Better Than Yours" as was evidenced by their division over leadership. Some followed Paul, some Peter, some Apollos, and others Christ (I Cor. 1:12). They played "Now I'll Get You" by suing one another in the pagan law courts (I Cor. 6:1-6). Sexual games were apparent in that one man was living with his father's wife, and no one seemed to care (I Cor. 5:1-5). Prostitution was singled out as a particular problem at Corinth (I Cor. 6:12-20). The game of "Alcoholic" was played at the Christians' "agape feasts" and celebrations of the Lord's Supper; "for in eating, each goes ahead with his own meal, and one is hungry and another is drunk" (I Cor. 11:21). Paul realizes that the freedom resulting from the experience of grace could, if misunderstood, lead to self-indulgence. But, Christian liberty is not a license to sin. It requires the updating of Child feelings in the Adult understanding that God is Love. "But I say, walk by the Spirit, and do not gratify the desires of the flesh. For the desires of the flesh are against the Spirit, and the desires of the Spirit are against the flesh; for these are opposed to each other, to prevent you from doing what you would. But if you are led by the Spirit you are not under the law" (Gal. 5:16-18).

Christian enthusiasm also gave rise to the gift of speaking in tongues (glossolalia). The release of Child feelings that accompanied faith in the gospel produced an outpouring of inarticulate sounds.[6] Paul claims to have spoken in tongues frequently (I Cor. 14:18). He does not attempt to repress this irrational expression among the Corinthian Christians but, on the contrary, sees it as a legitimate form of communication with God (I Cor. 14:2-5). This unintelligible outburst of Child feelings is welcomed as a religious expression, and Paul considers it unwise to bottle up these emotions. However, Paul insists that in public assemblies of the church someone be present to act as an interpreter of what is being said, so that the church may be edified and built up (I Cor. 14:28). If there were those who spoke in a tongue in the assembly, their number should be only two or at most three, and they should take turns in order to avoid utter confusion. Paul's position is that the release and expression of irrational Child feelings is permissible, but that Christians should update these feelings with respect to the Adult understanding of God's gift of OK-ness. "For if I pray in a tongue, my spirit prays but my mind is unfruitful. What am I to do? I will pray with the spirit and I will pray with the mind also; I will sing with the spirit and I will sing with the mind also" (I Cor. 14:14-15). To let Child feelings decommission the Adult would result in the church becoming Pandemonium rather than the Body of Christ—the dwelling place of the Holy Spirit. "Make love your aim, and earnestly desire the spiritual gifts, especially that you may prophesy" (I Cor. 14:1).

In his discussion of spiritual gifts, Paul describes love as the supreme gift of the Spirit that guides all other gifts in building up the community. Love frees the creative and affectionate energy of the Natural Child. "Love is patient and kind; love is not jealous or boastful; it is not arrogant or rude. Love does not insist on its own way; it is not irritable or resentful; it does not rejoice at wrong, but rejoices in the right. Love bears all things, believes all things, hopes all things, endures all things" (I Cor. 13:4-7). Love is the Adult way.

For Paul, life in the Spirit is more than feeling. It is an Adult way of behavior in which interpersonal transactions are mutually supportive. "Bear one another's burdens, and so fulfil the law of Christ" (Gal. 6:2). The power of the Spirit finds expression in considerate deeds. "The fruit of the Spirit is love, joy, peace, patience, kindness, goodness, faithfulness, gentleness, self-control; against such there is no law" (Gal. 5:23). *The Child feelings updated by the Adult realization that God is love constitutes the dynamic of the Spirit!*

The focus of Jesus' teaching is the nearness of the kingdom of God. "The nearness of God is the secret of Jesus' language about God as Father." [7] The presupposition of Jesus' ministry is that God is a merciful Father and men are called to accept and share his mercy. "Be merciful, even as your Father is merciful" (Luke 6:36). Life in the kingdom results in the freeing of the Natural

Child by the awareness that God is love. The disciples asked Jesus: "Who is the greatest in the kingdom of heaven?" (Matt. 18:1). Jesus calls a child and looking at him says: "Truly, I say to you, unless you turn and become like children, you will never enter the kingdom of heaven." It is the recognition of childlike dependence that is met and fulfilled by God's care that opens the Natural Child to the joy of living. "Whoever humbles himself like this child, he is the greatest in the kingdom of heaven."

In the Sermon on the Mount Jesus teaches his disciples that God is Father, and thus they are free from legal demands. This freedom does not grant irresponsibility but offers an opportunity to reflect the divine character in their own lives. "Let your light so shine before men, that they may see your good works and give glory to your Father who is in heaven" (Matt. 5:16). Knowledge of the Father who cares for the grass, the lilies, and the fallen sparrow, frees the disciple from basic anxiety (Matt. 6:25-33).

God as Father is the source of all life and knows the disciple's needs even before he asks (Matt. 6:8). The achievement of intimacy resulting from trusting God leads the disciple to pray "Our Father who art in heaven . . ." There is here expressed an openness and faith that the ultimate source of life is benevolent and that man is OK before God. Jesus taught his disciples to open their lives to a compassionate Father who will be sufficient for their needs in every situation. The early church lived according to the tradition of Jesus' prayer in Gethsemane: "Abba, Father, all things are possible to thee" (Mark 14:36).

The Lucan parable of the prodigal son presents an

artistic portrayal of the Father's love that makes one OK (Luke 15:11-32). The younger of two sons asks: "Father, give me the share of property that falls to me." Receiving his inheritance, the son goes into a foreign country and wastes his money. His funds depleted, he gets a job feeding swine. Thoughts turn homeward. There his father's servants have more than enough to eat; here he is slowly starving. He decides to return home and work in his father's house as a servant, convinced that he has forfeited his right to sonship. While the son is some distance from the house, his father catches sight of him and runs to him, embraces and kisses him. Before the son can complete his confession the father orders the best robe, shoes, and a ring for him. The fatted calf is killed and a banquet prepared. It is a time for celebration. This parable reveals the love of the Father who says to those feeling Not OK: "You're OK. Come let us eat and make merry." You now have permission to live as one who has discovered that God's love is the source of OK-ness. "My son was dead, but is alive again."

In the Gospel of John the gift of the Spirit also comes through acknowledging the love of God revealed in Jesus as the source of true life. The Father's love frees the believer from the darkness of Not-OK-ness and fills his life with the power to become a son of God (John 1:12-13). The promise of Jesus to his disciples is this: "If you love me, you will keep my commandments. And I will pray the Father, and he will give you another Counselor, to be with you for ever, even the Spirit of truth" (John 14:15-17). The Natural Child is liberated by the Word, which reveals love and grants peace (John 14:25-27). *The Spirit is the power of love grounded in God, revealed in Jesus, and shared in the community of believers.* These are the words of Jesus: "If you continue in my word, you are truly my disciples, and you will know the truth, and the truth will make you free" (John 8:31-32).

IX
The Call to Freedom

*For the law of the Spirit of life in Christ Jesus has set me free from
the law of sin and death.*

—Romans 8:2

We have outlined the comparison between the New
Testament's message of freedom and Transactional
Analysis's understanding of the solution to man's
Not-OK-ness. It is well here to summarize our findings
and to focus on the freedom that is potentially ours. The
call to freedom is a summons to live with security,
vitality, purpose, and joy. The future beckons with the
promise that <u>love is the source and destiny of human
existence</u>.

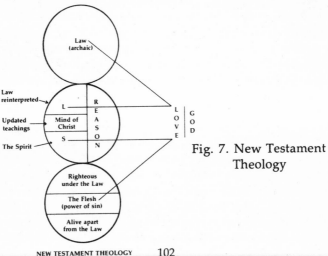

Fig. 7. New Testament
Theology

1. The experience of alienation or Not-OK-ness is universal and indelible; the feeling of estrangement is the result of separation from the source of our life. T.A. understands Not OK feeling as originating with the trauma of birth and infantile dependency. The biblical writers deal theologically with our experience of estrangement and trace its origin to the mythic Fall of Adam. Both T.A. and the New Testament concur in the understanding that our basic problem springs from the feelings of helplessness and dependence.

2. Not-OK Child feelings correspond to the condition of man as creature in biblical thought. For us to feel dependent is natural but does not constitute sin. These Not-OK Child feelings lead inevitably to the first emotional position: I'm Not OK—You're OK.

3. The feelings of Not-OK-ness prompt the little person to strive for survival and OK-ness. We all learn quite early to manipulate our world to satisfy our own needs. In time we improve our manipulative skills. These games produce an intensification of personal isolation and alienation. Trusting in our own ability to achieve OK-ness is sin—that is, missing the mark of trusting in the power of life beyond. Both the use and abuse of other people to relieve our burden of Not-OK-ness are sins.

4. The most serious and destructive of our games involve our efforts to manipulate God rather than to trust in him. The child learns early to obey his parents in order to receive positive strokes. The Parent ego state gradually transforms the Natural Child into the Adapted Child. The little person learns the script: "You can be OK, if . . ." This is the script of the legalist who strives to achieve God's approval by works of the law.

The result of legalism is to compound the experience of alienation because the Child conforms to the Parent without the benefit of the Adult.

5. The solution to the destructive script: "You can be OK, if . . ." is making an Adult faith-decision: "I'm OK." OK-ness is not achieved by conforming to Parent authority (law), but through realizing that *there is nothing in reality to justify the Not-OK Child feelings* (in other words, realization of grace). This is the reality to which T.A. points. The conviction that God accepts the sinner constitutes the heart of the Christian message of freedom. T.A.'s method precludes the making of specific statements about God, but T.A.'s analysis of man points beyond man to the gift of OK-ness as the fulfillment of life.

6. The I'm OK—You're OK position frees us to update Parent law in the Adult realization that God is love. Any authority that we are too insecure to examine intelligently constitutes Parent contamination and may be expressed by religious prejudice and dogmatism. The message of freedom in the New Testament is that God accepts the sinner; we are justified by a faith that is exclusive of the law.

7. The realization that Not-OK Child feelings are not justified in reality frees the Natural Child from Parent control. This release is accompanied by a surge of spiritual exuberance. Child feelings may then be updated in an Adult understanding that we are fundamentally OK. The Natural Child feelings of spontaneity, joy, affection, and creativity are to be cultivated. The feelings of fear, alienation, and insecurity are turned off as being inappropriate to the understanding that God is love.

8. The Christian continues to respond to new situations in the Adult understanding that love defines the interpersonal transactions that achieve intimacy. The mind of Christ relates to others so that God's love is shared. The sharing of love in the community of believers is the basis of the church's life (just as it is the basis of group therapy).

9. I keep in my office a poster given to me by my two daughters that is a caricature of T.A. On it is an elephant with his trunk in his ear repeating to himself "I'm OK, I'm OK, I'm OK." The experience of grace *is* that in which we stand; we continually reaffirm, "I'm OK." But, the therapeutic value of this affirmation rests in the full conviction that its constancy does indeed correspond to reality. The New Testament's proclamation of freedom is that God says in the Cross "You're OK." "Live as free men, yet without using your freedom as a pretext for evil; but live as servants of God" (I Peter 2:16).

Notes

Chapter I

1. B.F. Skinner, *Beyond Freedom and Dignity* (New York: Alfred A. Knopf, 1971), pp. 101–26.

2. Karl Menninger, *Whatever Became of Sin?* (New York: Hawthorn Books, 1973), p. 17.

3. Thomas A. Harris, *I'm OK—You're OK* (New York: Harper & Row, 1967), p. 236.

4. Walter Wink, *The Bible in Human Transformation* (Philadelphia: Fortress Press, 1973), pp. 1–15.

5. Rudolf Bultmann, *Jesus Christ and Mythology* (New York: Charles Scribner's Sons, 1958), pp. 45–59; "New Testament and Mythology," *Kerygma and Myth*, edited by H. W. Bartsch (New York: Harper Torchbooks, 1963), pp. 1–44.

6. Alvin Toffler, *Future Shock* (New York: Bantam Books, 1971), p. 358.

7. Rollo May, *Love and Will* (New York: Dell Publishing Co., 1969), p. 13–18. Compare May's description of the schizoid condition that he thinks "is a general tendency in our transitional age" (p. 16). Also see *Man's Search for Himself* (New York: New American Library, 1953, 1967), pp. 41–65.

Chapter II

1. Eric Berne, *Transactional Analysis in Psychotherapy* (New York: Grove Press, 1961), pp. 29–36; *Games People Play* (New York: Grove Press, 1964), pp. 23–24; *What Do You Say After You Say Hello?* (New York: Grove Press, 1972), pp. 11–21; Harris, pp. 16–36.

2. Murray T. Bloom, "Explorer of the Brain," *Reader's Digest*, LXXIII (July, 1958), p. 140. Also see W. Penfield,

NOTES

"Memory Mechanisms," *A.M.A. Archives of Neurology and Psychiatry*, LXIII (1952), pp. 178–98.

3. Harris, p. 11.

4. *Ibid.*, pp. 18–36.

5. Muriel James and Dorothy Jongeward, *Born to Win* (Menlo Park, Calif.: Addison-Wesley Publishing Company, 1971), pp. 127–37.

6. *Ibid.*, pp. 68–100; Berne, *What Do You Say?*, pp. 25–26.

Chapter III

1. Frederick Leboyer, *Birth Without Violence* (New York: Alfred A. Knopf, 1975), p. 17.

2. *Ibid.*, pp. 26–27.

3. *Ibid.*, p. 27.

4. Berne, *Games People Play*, p. 13.

5. Harris, p. 43.

6. Rudolf Bultmann, *Theology of the New Testament* (New York: Charles Scribner's Sons, 1955) I, 191.

7. Leboyer, p. 70.

8. Bultmann, II, 18.

Chapter IV

1. James and Jongeward, p. 133.

2. Everett L. Shostrom, *Man, the Manipulator* (New York: Bantam Books, published by arrangement with Abingdon, 1968), p. 3.

3. Berne, *Games People Play*, p. 15.

4. *Ibid.*, p. 48.

5. *Ibid.*

6. Leo Tolstoy, *The Death of Ivan Ilych* (New York: New American Library, 1960), p. 150.

7. Erich Fromm, *The Revolution of Hope* (New York: Bantam Books, 1968), p. 1. See also Rollo May's penetrating analysis of man in *Man's Search for Himself*, pp. 13–40.

107

8. Shostrom, pp. 12-14.

9. Harris, p. 225.

10. Karl Barth, *The Epistle to the Romans* (London: Oxford University Press, 1933), p. 51.

Chapter V

1. Harris, p. 45.

2. *Ibid.*, pp. 18–24.

3. See discussion of "The Little Lawyer" in Berne's *What Do You Say*, pp. 104–6.

4. *Ibid.* (Berne calls this legal thinking "cop-out" thinking, because the letter of the law is obeyed while its inner meaning is not.)

5. Gunther Bornkamm, *Jesus of Nazareth* (New York: Harper & Brothers, 1960), p. 104.

6. C. E. B. Cranfield, "St. Paul and the Law," *New Testament Issues*, edited by R. A. Batey (New York: Harper & Row, 1970), p. 149–50.

7. Thomas C. Oden, *Game Free* (New York: Harper & Row, 1974), p. 79–80.

Chapter VI

1. Harris, p. 50.

2. Oden, p. 83.

3. *Ibid.*, p. 84.

4. S. Vernon McCasland, *By the Finger of God* (New York: Macmillan, 1951).

5. William P. Blatty, *The Exorcist* (New York: Harper & Row, 1971), p. 218.

6. Fanita English, "TA: A Populist Movement," *Psychology Today*, VI (April, 1973), p. 50.

7. *Ibid.*

8. *Ibid.*

Chapter VII

1. Victor P. Furnish, *The Love Commandment in the New Testament* (Nashville: Abingdon, 1972), p. 150.

2. C. H. Dodd, *Gospel and Law* (New York: Columbia University Press, 1951), pp. 43–44.

3. Berne, *Transactional Analysis in Psychotherapy*, pp. 62–63.

4. Harris, p. 99.

Chapter VIII

1. Eric Berne, *Transactional Analysis in Psychotherapy*, pp. 47–50; and Harris, p. 99.

2. Harris, p. 233.

3. Fromm, pp. 13–14.

4. Muriel James and Louis M. Savary, *The Power at the Bottom of the Well* (New York: Harper & Row, 1974), p. 20.

5. Ernst Käsemann, *Jesus Means Freedom* (Philadelphia: Fortress Press, 1970), p. 54.

6. John K. Bontrager, *Free the Child in You* (Philadelphia: United Church Press, 1974), p. 110.

7. Bornkamm, p. 128.

Index of Biblical References